MAINE

Other books with a Maine flavor by

CHRISTIAN P. POTHOLM

available from National Book Network include:

Just Do It!: Political Participation in the 1990s
An Insider's Guide to Maine Politics
The Delights of Democracy
This Splendid Game

MAINE

The Dynamics of Political Change

CHRISTIAN P. POTHOLM

LEXINGTON BOOKS

A division of
ROWMAN & LITTLEFIELD PUBLISHERS, INC.
Lanham • Boulder • New York • Toronto • Oxford

LEXINGTON BOOKS

A division of Rowman & Littlefield Publishers, Inc.
A wholly owned subsidiary of The Rowman & Littlefield Publishing Group, Inc.
4501 Forbes Boulevard, Suite 200
Lanham, MD 20706

PO Box 317
Oxford
OX2 9RU, UK

British Library Cataloging in Publication Information Available

Library of Congress Cataloging-in-Publication Data

Potholm, Christian P., 1940–
Maine : the dynamics of political change / Christian P. Potholm.
p. cm.
Includes bibliographical references and index.
ISBN 0-7391-1332-1 (cloth : alk. paper) —
ISBN 0-7391-1333-X (pbk. : alk. paper)
1. Maine—Politics and government—1951– 2. Political culture—Maine. 3. Political participation—Maine. 4. Politics, Practical—Maine. I. Title.
JK2889.P68 2005
320.9741—dc22 2005020343

Printed in the United States of America

∞ ™ The paper used in this publication meets the minimum requirements of American National Standard for Information Sciences—Permanence of Paper for Printed Library Materials, ANSI/NISO Z39.48-1992.

"The past is fiction, the future is dream"

GRETEL EHRLICH

To Noah "No No" Potholm,
A new and bright star shining in our lives

TABLE OF CONTENTS

PART III: THE DYNAMICS OF PUBLIC REFERENDA

PART IV: THE DYNAMICS OF POLITICAL LEADERSHIP

PART V: THE DYNAMICS OF MAINE'S WELL-BEING

PART VI: MAINE IN COMPARATIVE PERSPECTIVE

PART VII: ONE WORD MORE

PREFACE

Maine politics is such an interesting and dynamic subject that it is hard to tell why so many people don't like it and don't really follow it, let alone participate in it. A fellow consultant, Jim Lukashevski, once told me that "democracy depends on the unconcern of the many" and maybe that is both true and normatively correct. Certainly Jim is on target when he says that in the real world of politics, one can't waste a lot of time on those who don't care enough even to register to vote.

Yet, as an educator, I have always tried to encourage students to become activists or at least to vote, or at the very least, in order to pass my course, go to polling places on election day and see the people who care enough about the Republic to take a few minutes out of their routine to vote.

Of course, I owe a great deal to those students and even to the deans to whom they sometimes complain about my making them follow and/or work on campaigns, candidate and ballot measures, with whom/which they disagree.

Teaching should be a very challenging business, one that keeps you young trying to answer their questions and put their concerns and opinions into a wider, longer or more balanced perspective. Although some professors claim to feel the tension between their Confucian side and their Taoist side, I never do and I always try to combine the two approaches to political wisdom.

Along the learning way, I have encountered some very interesting and informative students and they have left their mark on me, my teaching and my writings. *Maine: The Dynamics of Politics Change* is no exception. In particular, I would like to thank Sanida Kikuc, who came from war-torn Bosnia to make a new home and a new life, and while at Bowdoin, immersed herself in Maine politics enough to make a significant contribution to this book. Special kudos also to Tina Lin, whose final proofreading of the manuscript was so professional and helpful. Tina is a jewel.

And speaking of Bowdoin, kudos too should go to President Barry Mills, Dean Craig McEwen and the Government Department coordinator, Lynne Atkinson, all of whom have made The College both a more vibrant and user-friendly place.

I also want to repeat in this preface the names, and underscore the ongoing collaboration of those—Maria Fuentes, Erik Potholm and Sandra Quinlan Potholm—whom I have thanked so many times in previous volumes. They are a very vital personal focus group of three. Without their corrections, admonitions and significant input, my work would be more epigonic, less perspicacious and frankly more boring. I appreciate all the time and effort they have put in to help me try to communicate better.

Some others who provided stimulation, information and encouragement for various chapters and concepts include Dave Emery, Paul Mills, Greg Stevens, Jean Yarborough, Chris Hart, Dave Bunge, Mal Leary, Paul Franco, Janet Martin, John Oliver, Susan Tananbaum, Dennis Bailey, Lance Tapley, Dave Flannagan, Dick Morgan, Kim Mapps, Ann Mitchell, Pat Eltman, Kim Laramy, Bob Cott, George Campbell, Claire Quinlan, Corey Hascall, Keith Brown, Ethan Strimling, Richard Hornbeck, John Baldacci, Martha Freeman, Bonnie Washuk, Jana Kollias, Caren Epstein, Dick Barringer, Ande Smith, Mary Gamage, Bishop Geary, Mark Mutty, Pat Murphy, Lisa Gorman, Dick Mullins, Alexis Bawden, Olympia Snow, Phil Harriman, Dana Connors and Dan Levine.

Also, Jill Ryan, Rick Mullins, Steve Cerf, A.J. Higgins, Peter Cianchette, Abby Holman, Kay Rand, John Turner, Angus King, George Smith, Edith Leary, Joy O'Brien, Mingus Mapps, Leon Gorman, Jock McKernan, Solveig Christensen, Mike Michaud, Bob Clifford, Les Otten, Alison Bennie, Tom Daffron, Linda Hornbeck, Dana Lee, Brian Clement, Larry Benoit, John Quinlan, Scott Hood, Heather Potholm Mullins, Allen

Springer, Chris Lockwood, Jerry Bernier, Chris Duval, Frank Chi, Anna Mullins, Chris Williams, Patty Ames, Bishop Malone, Stephanie Hart, Tony Buxton and Richard Paraday.

A special thanks also to Jed Lyons and his very able staff at Lexington Books, especially MacDuff Stewart and Audrey Babkirk, who have provided such fine editorial input for this and other books of mine. Jed remains an insider's insider when it comes to Maine and national politics and his insights never fail to intrigue and stimulate.

CPP
Otter Brook Cove

INTRODUCTION

Was Heraclitis right? The Greek philosopher stated that you can never put your foot in the same river twice because the river is always changing. Change, he said, was the essence of the universe.

Is the river of Maine politics never the same from one moment to the next? Is it always a different river each time you step into it? Or are there patterns and processes which, if understood, can foretell future political outcomes, a metaphysical sameness that allows for prediction as well as analysis?

I have been fortunate to have been actively involved in politics since 1968 and the presidential campaign effort of Senator Eugene McCarthy, and have studied the political process for even longer. Moreover, I have had the wonderful opportunity to move back and forth from classroom to political arena, from scholarship of and about political figures to the nuts and bolts of all kinds of election situations from U.S. Senators to mayors as well as a host of ballot measure and issue advocacy campaigns in several dozens states.

I have always been fascinated by the ebb and flow of politics. Not the policies which follow or precede elections but the dynamics of the electoral process. To me, the answer to the question about commonality is simple: there are common aspects to politics in Maine which, if understood, can help us grasp both the significance and insignificance of various discrete political phenomena.

There is value in a holistic approach to the dynamism of politics which transcends the moment by moment, "instant" analysis now so popular on cable television and talk radio. The dynamics of political change can be observed and explained, not just after the fact, when everything is "clear," but in the middle of the action. Political campaigns have observable and predictable ebbs and flows and interactions which can, even as events are unfolding, give us a sense of what is to come.

This volume is based on that premise and since most of the pieces were written in the middle of the action, or just following certain key events, it is possible to gain a deeper understanding of both the process as it was occurring and the why's of the outcomes.

Strangely enough, many, if not most, political reporters are not interested in these deeper realities. Neither are their editors. Since the editors give the directions, it is perhaps not so surprising that political reporters aren't that interested in in-depth analysis. In thirty-five years of following Maine politics, I can count on one hand the number of political reporters who have engaged in substantive discussions about the why's and wherefores of a particular campaign. All is of and for the moment.

Gone too are the days when political reporters were supposed to figure out campaign dynamics. Now there is only "instant" analysis based on the day's events—or more likely—the latest poll. Most editors are too interested in pushing their or their paper's particular agenda to care much one way or the other about campaign realities. They wish to exhort, to pontificate, to "drive the ballot" but not understand the psychographics or even the demographics of the possible outcomes in any given political situation.

There are really only two major types of political reporters in Maine, usually depending on which type of paper they work for.

There are the major daily political reporters who are very establishment oriented, they virtually always go with the conventional wisdom (up until that wisdom is overridden by events) and give the nod to both incumbents and whatever ballot measure is perceived to be ahead in the newspaper polls of the day.

Then there are a few counterculture reporters, usually who write for weekly newspapers, who are anti-establishment with mind-numbing regularity and who like to throw verbal bombs and express their personal ideologies and preferences but don't often take an objective look at how likely a political phenomenon is to last or disappear.

For those who follow, even tangentially, the political activities of the Pine Tree state, a combination of the two is likely to be more satisfying and historically valid. It is in this direction I hope that *Maine: The Dynamics of Political Change* moves and moves smartly.

Here are the basic assumptions or hypotheses which I try to highlight in this work:

History is malleable. In political campaigns, one side wins and the other side loses but nothing is pre-ordained and guaranteed to happen. "Part I: The Dynamics of an Open Seat" begins by focusing on the most wide open of election situations, where two or more contenders do not have to struggle against an entrenched incumbent who has all of the advantages of incumbency, funds, media access and the presumption of invincibility which editors of newspapers often confer on them.

Elections are often decided by the quality of one campaign versus the quality of another. This does not mean that any incumbent can be beaten by any challenger or any cause defeated by any other; but it does mean that any incumbent can run a poor campaign and be defeated by an excellent effort by her or his opponent.

This aspect of the campaign qua campaign lies at the heart of my analysis of Maine elections and in the chapters which follow, I try to show the reader critical tipping points in various campaigns.

"Part II: The Dynamics of the Campaign Process" seeks to capture the essence of political change *as it is happening*. Given the changing nature of politics, it is harder and harder for the average citizen to see state politics changing before their eyes.

This was not always the case. As late as the 1970's, it was possible to wage campaigns which "made" news and therefore generated momentum other than that produced by the 30 second TV commercial. Bill Cohen's walk across Maine in 1972 was one such campaign as was Dave Emery's in 1974 and, of course, Jim Longley's surprising successful run as Maine's first Independent governor occurred because of the vigorous nature of his press and day to day campaign efforts.

Today, many political reporters often engage in self-fulfilling prophecies. Most never go out onto the campaign trail to see how the countryside is responding to campaign A or B. Also, many do not understand polling and take the various head to head match ups as "givens" as well as "predictors." In my experience, most are led astray by one simple aspect of polling, how to understand a basic head to head match up between two candidates. In my thirty five years in Maine politics dealing with reporters, I have found it extremely difficult to get most of them—one major exception is Mal Leary—to look beyond the surface numbers of that head to head.

For example, if you take most challengers, they are less well known than the incumbents they face. Therefore, in order to get an accurate assessment of the potential for the challenger, one needs to look at the match up ONLY among those voters who ALREADY know both candidates. Media polls never show this dimension in their stories. Reporters almost never look at this dimension even when the poll is in their own paper. Therefore they quite often miss the developing story.

For example, when Angus King began his run against Joe Brennan in 1994, Brennan had a huge lead among all voters and, indeed, nonvoters. This was simply because Angus King was hardly known at all, with fewer than 12% of voters even knowing who he was. Therefore, it was imperative to look at the much smaller cohort to see what those voters who knew both candidates thought. In this subgroup, even a year before the election, King led. Try as I might, I could never convince many working reporters that Brennan's lead was artificial and would evaporate if all or most voters got to know both men. I am not aware of any reporter who thought Angus King would be elected governor.

The same thing was true in the last gubernatorial campaign which pitted the virtually unknown Peter Cianchette against the almost universally known John Baldacci. Even a full year before the election of 2002, among most likely voters who knew both men, it was a virtual dead heat. Nevertheless, the popular newspaper polls in the beginning of the race showed Baldacci with a huge 25+% lead due to his name recognition. Everybody knew him, only one in five knew his challenger.

Virtually every reporter I spoke to during that campaign insisted that Baldacci would win and win big. They refused to pay any attention to the actual predictor cohort, voters who knew both. That is why during the last weeks of the campaign, the *Portland Press Herald* and *Bangor Daily News* both published polls showing Baldacci with a 20% lead. Both papers were happy to write off the Republican Peter Cianchette. Both editorialized vigorously for Baldacci.

Yet, the "know both candidates" cohort put the race virtually within the margin of error and on election day, Baldacci did win, of course, but by a very much smaller margin (6%), than the newspaper polls had predicted. If a candidate wins by 6%, that means that a swing of just 3.1% of voters would have turned the election around.

As we indicate in a subsequent chapter, this is exactly what Cianchette supporters hoped Governor King would provide. His action, or as it turned out, "inaction," was a major factor in the outcome. That is because although by October, 2002, over 85% of Republicans were lining up for Cianchette, and 85% of Democrats for Baldacci, Independents were going in great numbers for Baldacci.

Many insiders believed then, and believe now, that had King endorsed Cianchette, the outcome would have been different since contemporary polling data showed that three out of four Independents in October 2002 said an endorsement of either candidate would have made a difference to them.

The fact of the matter is that candidates in the twenty-first century in Maine live and die by TV. Gone are the days of true retail politics. The state is too big, the population too diverse and the newspaper and TV coverage too superficial to make an impact any other way than with ones own paid TV ads.

Therefore, and this is the key variable, since TV ads determine the course of most campaigns in Maine, and since a candidate's ability to affect the course depends on their ability to raise money to get on TV, misunderstood public polls can shut off a challenger's funds readily and often nearly complexly. So by following polls which are reading the past rather than the future, many campaigns hit stone walls.

Part II tries to capture the various moments when one campaign breaks out and another collapses.

Ballot measures are different from candidate elections. This is by now a truism of Maine politics. Yet many candidates and others, including some political insiders, attempt to apply the lessons of candidate politics to ballot measures. For example, especially if you are a challenger, you want to get your name recognition up. This means you want to "make news" by putting out press releases and having press conferences. You want people to know who you are and a free wheeling press conference is often a way to generate news at six pm or eleven on TV and in the newspapers the next day.

By contrast, ballot measures are determined almost entirely by the paid media and the way you avoid press conferences and keep reporters out of the information stream since they invariably will treat any ballot measure campaign development as a "he said, she said" phenomenon. Press accounts of events in ballot measures are almost always balanced with side one getting about the same amount of coverage as the other. If you are behind, you can't afford to have the opposition staying "equal" with you and if you are ahead, you don't want to give the opposition equal time. Therefore in ballot measures, one tries to avoid situations which give opponents an equal chance to present their messages, you much prefer the 30 second commercial which you control completely.

"Part III: The Dynamics of Pubic Referenda" takes an in-depth look at the process by which public policy is made in Maine at the ballot box. So its various chapters look at demographics, at psychographics and about the interplay among various forces in the ballot measure context. The most important among them are often cast in sharp relief by what is called "segmentation analysis," whereby the electorate in any given campaign situation is broken up into discernable—and trackable—portions.

In Maine ballot measure politics, certain groups remain important—even vital—segments no matter what the issue or what the era. Some are simply more important that others in election after election. For example, in the campaigns of which I am a part, I always say if I can win 55% of the Franco American vote and 55% of the women in the home vote, I will be successful nine out of ten campaigns. That's about the percentage I have averaged in Maine.

Yet in 2004, in the struggle to keep Maine's bear hunting on a scientific even keel, we were unable to get 55% of either the Franco American or women in the home vote, but managed to win by getting 55% of the women who work outside the home and over 65% of males. There is change on the campaign trail and one has to stay away from formulae if they are not working in a particular case.

Maine has very high standards for political leadership. We are a small state in terms of population and a poor state in terms of our economic and geographical location within the American economic system. But we have high, even "wicked" high standards for our political figures. Unlike citizens in other states, we don't expect our elected officials to enrich themselves at the public trough. And, as far as our elected officials in Washington, we don't expect them to raid the federal treasury on our behalf.

But we do expect "independence" and "strong leadership" and a sensitivity to "Maine values." "Part IV: The Dynamics of Political Leadership" looks as these virtues in operation and tries to explore the way Maine people make their political choices. In this regard, I have included several pieces about presidential politics simply because the way Mainers judge presidential candidates often mirrors exactly the way we choose and the reasons we choose our other officials.

What has proven fascinating to me in researching this phenomenon is its longevity. What Maine people expect in 2006 is what they expected in 1948 and 1848. It's quite amazing really!

Maine politics are underpinned by our sense of well-being. I have sampled public opinion in all of the 48 contiguous states and I have never found citizens of other states to be as positive about their own state as Mainers. No matter how much Maine people may complain about the weather, the economic hardship or anything else, in the law of large numbers, they remain steadfast in their love for the state. Their own inner landscapes reflect the sense of well-being they feel at the notion that they are in and of Maine.

"Part V: The Dynamics of Maine's Well-Being" explores some of the dimensions of that well-being, both personal and collective. Sharing some experiences, projecting some values and trying to capture the essence of what being in Maine really means, this section tries to look behind the political dynamics to view the various Maines and the way they shape our cognitive maps.

There is sadness here, of course, as well as joy, tragedy as well a triumph and some unexpected danger signs which could threaten our political well-being in the future. So there are several essays on these dimensions.

Mainers are a people blessed. But on balance, we in Maine consider ourselves blessed by our location and our sense of values. "Part VI: The Dynamics of Maine in Comparative Perspective" seeks to put our situation in perspective and look at other political situations for comparison. It also attempts to trace the well springs of our political system back to the earliest beginnings of the American political system, now all too fashionably written off by some as simply an imperfect democracy dominated by slave-holding white males.

Our early Republic did have these features but it had much, much more, a character of leadership which set in motion the political framework by which an increasingly free society operated within a basic framework which was both majestic and *sui generis*.

Strictly speaking, there was no independent "Maine" then, but there is now and it is good to celebrate its essence. In the pages which follow we hope to share its political and psychological dimensions in all their dynamism.

Taken together, I hope this volume will enrich the lives of those who take the time to explore the political realities of "Maine: The Way Political Life Should Be."

I

THE DYNAMICS OF AN OPEN SEAT

INTRODUCTION

Nothing is more prized in politics than an open seat. It opens up a myriad of possibilities for one and all. An open seat is the Holy Grail of American politics since it happens so rarely.

In the United States House of Representatives, incumbents win over 90% of the time. This is approximately the turnover rate in the Tanzanian and old Soviet Union parliaments!

Races for governor or senator are equally stacked in favor of the incumbents. Therefore students of politics want to pay particular attention to the highly competitive races, especially those with a non-incumbent situation.

The essays which follow try to capture the key moments in campaigns which are seldom chronicled. Also, since whoever wins tends to be regarded as having somehow been assured of winning, there is little attention paid to the might have beens of a particular race.

Here, then, are glimpses into the Maine 2002 races for the open second Congressional seat and the open governor's position in Maine. For comparison purposes, I also have included a contemporary look at the first term incumbency re-election of Senator Susan Collins, a race in which she was perceived to be highly vulnerable by Maine's largest daily newspaper.

Taken together, these chapters capture Maine politics at many levels, especially the intertwined nature of campaign dynamics, personality and the psychographic interactions which give campaigns their substance and process.

IN PRAISE OF VIRGINS

Just when supporters of Senator Susan Collins were resting easy thinking that her opponent in the general election of 2002 would be the very liberal Chellie Pingree, along comes the news that there will be another candidate in the Democratic primary.

Robert "Bob" Dunfey, long time Democratic activist and fundraiser and heir to one of Maine's most prominent Democratic families, is off and running. As a former businessman and considerably more moderate in his issue profile, Dunfey would be a far more serious challenge to the junior senator as he brings centrist positions on issues such as gun control and small business.

Moreover, he has already brought together a most formidable campaign team, one with national credentials, one able to go toe-to-toe with the professionals of the Pingree effort. His pollster is the well-known Tom Keily from Boston, the national Democratic pollster with the most experience in Maine.

Dunfey's campaign manager is the talented Joshua Bouvair of Main Street Strategies who brings a good deal of grass roots and direct mail experience and whose association with Winning Directions brings the Dunfey campaign considerable intellectual and campaign resources at the national level. This grass roots activism on the part of Dunfey will have to be countered vigorously by the Pingree forces who will need to engage the extremely successful Joe Cowie to organize her grassroots and local get out the vote effort. Cowie is often behind the scenes in many successful local, state and national efforts.

Perhaps even more significant is Dunfey's choice of media firms. Hank Sheinkopf has a national reputation having done media work for Clinton/Gore in 1996. Insiders feel confident that Sheinkopf is not coming to Maine to play patty-cake politics and would not be coming at all unless he believed he had a good chance to be part of a winning team. If Sheinkopf can work some electronic magic, six months from now, Congressmen Baldacci and Allen may want to reevaluate their premature support of Pingree.

Not that Pingree will roll over and play dead. She has her own strong team of consultants led by Will Robinson. Will Robinson, of McWilliams, Cosgrove and Robinson, will duel Sheinkopf on behalf of Pingree. Robinson was the media savant whose grainy and realistic images earned Gay Rights supporters their first—and only—statewide victory in Maine during the 1995 election cycle. His "Lobster Boy" commercial won that battle and remains a classic of a powerful, mind changer commercial. Robinson is a force to be reckoned with as well and his presence clearly points up just how the Democratic senatorial primary in 2002 will be a battle of heavy weights.

Given Pingree's $300,000 war chest and the considerable fundraising talents of Anna Lidman (who was a big factor in the successful Turnpike Widening referendum of 1996, raising over $800,000 for that endeavor), Dunfey will have to bring considerable personal and national financial support to make this a race. It is said he will have a considerable war chest and the support of the Kennedy family, especially Patrick Kennedy. Dunfey's father was head of the Maine effort for John F. Kennedy in 1960, so these ties are of long standing.

Best of all to my way of thinking, Dunfey has never run for political office—major or otherwise. To many, that may seem a negative. But to me, it is a positive. Since there is a right way, a wrong way, a candidate's way and a consultant's way (and they are seldom synonymous!), I have always preferred candidates with less electoral experience, not more. Certainly, when it comes to high electoral office, experience is vastly overrated. Bill Cohen was mayor of Bangor and a member of the city council but had never run outside his home city and Angus King had never run for public office, to give but the most prominent examples.

In fact, over the years, I have concluded that state senators and representatives almost always make poor candidates because having run in their immediate areas, they develop styles and assumptions which cannot be extrapolated to the larger congressional district or state wide level. Indeed, the history of Democratic and Republican primaries has been the history of broken dreams for former state representatives and senators.

Give me a campaign virgin anytime.

The candidacy of Bob Dunfey may not be good news for the Pingree or Collins camps. But it is great news for political junkies. The Democratic 2002 senatorial primary promises to be spirited, exciting and run by professionals with national reputations. They will cover up a lot of the candidates' inexperience and mistaken assumptions. The coming primary will be poll and media driven as well as having an amusing grass roots sideshow.

This is shaping up as a major match-up of political consulting talent, a feast of gunfighters at the Maine OK Corral.

It will be a major and engaging battle.

It will be lots of fun to watch.

A WHOLE NEW BALL GAME

January has seen a sea change in the second C.D. race for the Democratic nomination. John Nutting's surprisingly strong fundraising effort has changed the dynamics of that race. With each having $150,000 on hand, he and Mike Michaud are the only ones in the race with sufficient cash on hand to make a dramatic, early strike on television.

Moreover, insiders are very impressed that he was able to raise so much money through his own efforts. But for John Nutting, after a lifetime of pitching cow manure twice a day, fund raising may seem child's play. Veteran observers call him relentless in his search for money and support.

Such a vigorous financial challenge to Michaud was unexpected. Most party regulars did not anticipate Nutting's ability to keep pace with Michaud, nor did they expect his "pro-business, pro-environment" message to catch on among party regulars outside Nutting's own state senate district. Michaud, however, has been making important strides on his own and his districtwide organization would still seem to give him a decided edge on the ground.

Nutting has signed up a strong professional team to help him spend his money. Alan Seacrest is a well-known and respected Democratic pollster and Murphy Putnam is a Washington media firm of note. This is clearly to be a campaign of both substance and style, not just a one trick pony of "the only working farmer in the race."

Michaud's media guru, Tom Opel, also knows New England and may provide solid guidance on how to sell the former President of the Maine Senate on TV. Selling former presidents of the Maine senate on TV is now something of a struggling cottage industry, however, having thus far proven a major challenge for the media firms of Duke Dutremble and Mark Lawrence. One can only hope that Opel, also being Tom Dashele's media maven, will not bring echoes of that smarmy snake oil salesman to Maine.

Some are making much of the fact that Murphy Putnam is also the media firm selected by John Baldacci in his run for governor. This is quite a break with Baldacci's and Larry Benoit's administrative assistant's long standing policy of not letting "their" media firm work for another candidate in the state.

When George Campbell, for example, ran for Congress in 1994, Baldacci's team forced their media firm to choose between the underdog challenger Campbell and the incumbent Baldacci. As angry as Campbell and his supporters were, the choice was easy for the media firm in question.

To capture the center/right, both Nutting and Michaud will have to contest for the support of the outdoor hunting and fishing segment of the Democratic electorate, a segment often overlooked by "liberal" or "progressive" candidates. In this regard, a preprimary endorsement by SAM could prove decisive in determining which man gets the most votes.

But enough of the two fundraising leaders. There is another way to look at Nutting's recent momentum. There are only so many "moderate" and "conservative" voters in the Democratic second CD primary and it now appears that a strong Nutting could, in fact, hold Michaud's vote total down by splitting that "moderate" vote. Throw in Dave Costello and you have three moderate/conservative Democrats fighting for the same bloc of votes.

In this scenario, neither Nutting nor Michaud would emerge victorious but both would lose to any Democrat who captured the bulk of the "progressive" or "liberal" portion of that vote.

In terms of cash on hand, Lori Handrahan, Susan Longley and Sean Faircloth are the current front runners for that segment of the "progressive" vote. But only Handrahan ($113,000 on hand) and Longley ($77,000 on hand) seem in a position to challenge Michaud and Nutting in a sustained air war. Longley has the edge in name recognition and Handrahan the ability to throw in another $100,000 if she begins to gain traction. Faircloth is a hard worker and his campaign is certainly currently winning the press release war but with only $36,000 on hand, he is in danger of being outgunned all across the political spectrum.

Faircloth's problem remains that he must do well against Michaud in Penobscot and southern Aroostok while still making a respectable showing in Lewiston against Nutting, Michaud and Longley as well as former Lewiston mayor Kaileigh Tara. Tara has been held back by her mayoral duties but she plans a people's campaign to negate the spending advantages of the other candidates.

With so many candidates running major league campaigns, the 14,000 or so Democratic voters are in for a real treat as the primary heats up. Any of four or five candidates could win and the race remains very much up for grabs.

Democratic insiders in all camps continue to tell me that the primary will be won "on the ground" with grassroots efforts being the deciding factor. I remain skeptical. I believe the second District Democratic nomination will go to whoever has the best—and most sustained—TV air war.

Maybe with a little help from the ground game.

Postscript: "Live by the 30 second commercial, die by the 30 second commercial" is an old but very telling political adage. In this race for an open seat nomination, it turned out to be very true. The end of the Democratic primary season saw Michaud, Longley and Faircloth with strong TV efforts. Nutting's final blitz, however, featured a 30 second spot showing him dressed in a black suit hanging around a school playground and denied admission to the bus full of children by a vigilant female bus driver. I'm still trying to figure out the point of that "closer" ad. So too apparently are Democratic primary voters, for after a very strong start, Nutting finished a distant fourth with only 12% of the vote.

CAMPAIGN IN 3D

We are now beginning to see the shape of the governor's race cast in much sharper relief. It is going to be a close, hotly contested race. It's going to be race with "3D" dimensions.

Jonathan Carter's qualification for the so-called "Clean Elections" money, some $900,000, has thrown some Democrats into near panic. And well it should. With that kind of money and a sensible, progressive centrist message, Carter could hit 20% of the vote. He could go even higher if the other candidates make major mistakes. When not sounding shrill and didactic, Carter can be charming and persuasive. He has a lot of upside potential if he runs a smart campaign.

So the Democrats are motivated to pull out all the stops and try to get him thrown off the ballot. Carter could cost them the governor's race and they have a 30 year tradition of trying to get those who can cost them that prize off the ballot.

It was in 1970, when Governor Ken Curtis trailed Republican Jim Erwin by as much as 28 points in their race. Curtis had just survived an unpleasant primary against Plato Truman who had focused on Curtis' income tax policy with great effect. When Truman lost in the Democratic primary in June, he then registered as an Independent (this is no longer allowed).

Only tough muscling by the Democratic state chair Severin Belliveau and other Democrat stalwarts kept Truman out of the general election and enabled Curtis to win one of the closest governor's races in Maine history.

Carter and the Greens, by drawing from the "progressive" wing of the Democratic party have—in the minds of some Democrats—already cost them several important races. These include most notably Pat McGowan in 1992 when Carter got 9% and McGowan lost by 7% against Olympia Snowe and again with Joe Brennan in 1994 when Carter got 6% and Brennan only lost by 2% against Angus King. Incidentally, Carter did very well that year in Brennan's old senate district and on Munjoy Hill, getting 15% of that vote.

Most amusing, the *Portland Press Herald*, which has abandoned all objectivity early and become deeply involved in promoting Chellie Pingree for the U.S. Senate and John Baldacci for governor—with their reporting as well as their editorial page support—recently called the Democrat shenanigans "a healthy part of the competitive system of elections"!

Even more gratuitously, the *Press Herald* warned Carter: "Now that he's swimming with the sharks, the Green candidate will be treated like chum." Such a violent metaphor for a political race from such a liberal paper! One is shocked, just shocked!

But even more astute Democrats see that there are now really three Democrats in the general election contest for governor.

Dave Flanagan's early follies gave them hope that this conservative Democrat—recently turned Independent—would drop out of the race or at least not run a viable campaign because he wouldn't use his own money.

But Flanagan has now turned to his own resources to keep his fragile campaign in the race. Look for him to go on television very soon to try to catch up with Carter. He must do that in order to stay viable for the fall. If he trails Carter on Labor Day, even the staunchest Brennanistas may throw up their hands and stay home.

Today, Flanagan remains the best hope for those Brennan supporters who do not want Baldacci to win to ensure his defeat. By voting for this recent Democrat, they can keep Baldacci from winning but not abandon their Democratic roots. Flanagan's somewhat conservative Democratic status thus has some appeal to those Democrats who now find Baldacci too liberal and too close to the AFL CIO as well as too responsible for Joe's loss to Susan Collins in 1996.

Flanagan continues to have problems however. His new campaign slogan seems made for true cognitive dissonance. "Stay Independent" is an obvious attempt to capitalize on the continuing popularity of Angus King and suggests that Flannagan is "independent" too.

Unfortunately, the folks at www.opensecrets.org have been doing some research on their own. Flanagan's Democrat donations are now a matter of public record. And what a record it is! In the past four election cycles, Flanagan gave nearly $12,000 to a string of Democratic candidates including Al Gore, Mark Lawrence, Tom Allen, Jim Mitchell, John Baldacci (3 times!), Janet Mills, Tom Andrews, George Mitchell, Jim Tierney, Joe Brennan, Dale McCormick and Duke Dutremble as well as the Maine Democratic State Committee.

Quite a pattern of "independence."

Seems like a pretty loyal Democrat to me.

Now it is true that when head of CMP, David did give $250 to Bill Cohen and $1250 to Olympia Snowe—but then he turned around and gave Mark Lawrence $1500 as if to cancel out that stain on his Democratic honor!

Honestly, I will never understand what any donors are thinking about when they give both sides money in a campaign. Don't they know the candidates will check to see if their opponents got money too? Don't they know the contempt most candidates have when somebody tries to cover all the bases? It's all very strange.

The upshot of all this is that Republicans are now taking heart. There are three candidates who will all draw from the same behavioral Democratic spectrum. From here on, John Baldacci will have to try to fight to hold his base against "Democratic" challenges from the left and the right.

John Baldacci's problems are just beginning.

THE PERFECT STORM

Quite a few readers have asked if Maine's political TV season is different this year. It certainly is and will continue to be right through the election.

There is currently an unprecedented amount of "soft money" floating around in the system. Both the national Democrats and Republicans are awash with it. There are tens of millions of dollars sitting in Washington just waiting to flow out to the states for use in important races.

All the accent on the so-called "Clean Elections" money, which has put $900,000 in the hands of Jonathan Carter, has distracted most political observers from the unprecedented storm of soft money ads now being broadcast on behalf of various candidates. No political ad storm of this magnitude has ever hit Maine before.

What accounts for this storm of activity?

For the state of Maine, a number of factors have come together to produce our current perfect storm of political TV advertising. First, there is the total amount of money available at the national level, raised in haste and love, as the parties try to stay ahead of the pace of campaign finance reform. Both parties have more money to spend on state races then they've ever had before.

Second, this unprecedented amount of money comes at a time when there is a perceived need on the part of the national parties to influence the voters in many states. With both the U.S. House and the Senate in play for this election cycle, the Democrats and Republicans are extremely anxious to tip the balances wherever and whenever they can. Both parties see that they could capture both houses of Congress. Both parties see that situation as a zero-sum game, whereby they could win it all in an off-year election and set themselves up for the presidential election of 2004.

The third element of the current perfect storm is the relative cost of TV in Maine. A thousand gross rating point buy statewide—enough for everyone in the state to see any commercial eight or nine times—costs about $125,000. Believe it or not, this is very cheap by national standards and both parties are looking for the best bang for their buck. It is so much cheaper to maximize soft money's impact in a place like Maine than in Ohio or New Jersey or California and with competitive races in Maine, the state looks like a very good buy in terms of cost effectiveness.

Nationally, Maine is in play.

We have the open seat in the second Congressional District now occupied by John Baldacci. His decision to run for governor puts his seat at risk for the Democrats and encourages the Republicans to think they can gain a vital net pickup. That is why voters in southern Maine are already seeing a barrage of ads on behalf of Kevin Raye and Mike Michaud. In no other second CD race in our political history has there been so much Portland TV so early for both candidates. Usually only one candidate from the district has enough money for much Portland TV and never in Maine history have both candidates been able to be on with such volume in October, let alone September.

The U.S. Senate race showed this phenomenon even earlier. Democrat ads from Washington, from both the AFL-CIO and national Democratic party, started advertising heavily in July for Chellie Pingree. However ineffective they might have been in changing the relative position of the two candidates, they provoked a markedly increased rate of spending by the national Republicans. There has been a flood of ads on behalf of Pingree and Collins ads put on by the national parties.

But there has also been a huge amount of candidate ads as well, adding to our perfect storm of TV ads. Viewers have probably seen more U.S. Senate ads by October 1 than they would normally see during the entire election in normal times. Although that race seems to have settled into a solid 2–1 for Collins, there is no sign that the national Democrats will stop the soft money third party ads for Pingree. Pingree's own pollster claims the race is much closer and besides, the national Democrats are not likely to pull the plug on any woman senatorial candidate, especially one running in a cheap TV state. Look for the Senate race to keep adding to the perfect storm right up until Election Day.

The governor's race, too, has added to the perfect storm. During August, there were days and weeks in which the third party, issue advocacy and national and state party ads actually exceeded the number of ads paid for by the candidates. During the week of September 12–18, for example, the Democratic party ads were virtually half of the total for Baldacci and the Republican party ads were more than half of the total for Cianchette. In thirty years, I have never seen this pattern hold for more than a few days, and that usually only during the last weekend.

In addition, as many of you have undoubtedly noticed, whenever the hurricane winds from the Maine races die down—even for a moment—there is a huge inrush of hot air and truly acid rain from New Hampshire!

As with most big storms there isn't much you can do about it, so just sit back and enjoy the howling wind and pelting rain.

The perfect storm has a month to blow.

A GRAND MOMENT

It was a grand moment in Maine political history. No matter what your party affiliation or personal preference, it was a historic and welcome event.

Mike Michaud did it.

Mike Michaud did what no recognizable Franco American had ever done before. He became the first openly Franco American to be elected to Congress or the U.S. Senate. In doing do, he broke a decades long tradition of political discrimination, both within the Democratic party and the entire electorate. He also overcame what has become known as "the curse of the Francos," whereby members of that community are allowed "to do well but not too well."

Mike Michaud not only did well, he did very well.

There were a number of obstacles to his historic achievement.

First, roughly $4 million was spent on negative ads. Two million came from the Republican congressional committee, and two million came from the Democratic congressional committee but all blended together to sour the political process and make the voters angry. They could have taken their anger out on him.

Second, he had major, very credible opposition, not just in the general election but in his Democratic primary as well. Kevin Raye was a very appealing, energetic and talented foe (unfortunately for him, some of his appeal blunted by those terrible DC ads the RNC put on) and Susan Longley, John Nutting, Sean Faircloth, David Costello and Lori Handrahan all provided very viable alternatives to the voters. Michaud overcame them all, not with ease and not with simple name ID but with a strong sense of self and a positive attitude toward the future.

Interestingly enough, as the campaign was beginning, Michaud joined many others candidates in attending a large Bowdoin candidate forum. He arrived a half hour early, was extremely well prepared, met with all the student groups and gave a very polished and forceful presentation.

Many students were highly impressed and when the class voted on "the candidate most likely to succeed," they chose him. It was an early "straw in the wind," but one which proved to be telling.

For the Franco Americans, Michaud's election is an accomplishment of note. The Franco Americans, who make up 18% of Maine's voting population, have long been a key swing vote in our politics. Ever since 1972 and the elimination of the straight party ticket choice, the Francos have been "in play," responding to Republican and Independent candidates as well as their traditional favorites, the Democrats. But despite their importance to both the Democrat's nominating process and the general election, they have long been denied their proper place in the political firmament.

Even when the Democrats have nominated talented Franco Americans, such as Elmer Violette for Congress in the second CD (1972) or Duke Dutremble for Congress in the first CD (1994), the Democrats in general, and the Franco American community in particular, have not given these candidates their full support.

But Mike Michaud changed all that.

From Lewiston to Ft. Kent, he held the Franco vote solid, running up substantial majorities in all the places he had to carry. And although Raye nearly won—and would have without the enormous turnout boost given Michaud in the host of blue collar, mill towns from Skowhegan to Rumford to Millinocket—Michaud ran an effective campaign, a winning blend of good TV and stupendously good GOTV. He kept the Democrats at home, picked up Republican support in the mill towns and he led the ticket, helping to boost John Baldacci's plurality.

He deserves his victory. Mike is one of the nicest people I've ever met in politics and one of the hardest working. He has served his state 22 years, first in the Maine House, then the Senate and finally as Senate President. Through hard work, dedication and self-improvement, he has made himself into a first rate candidate and he improved weekly on the campaign trail. At the same time, Michaud has always been true to himself and his core values.

He is an unusual blend of confidence and humility. Eager to learn and yet well grounded, he projects a very appealing image, an image which mirrors the reality of who he was, who he is and who he will become. Ideological, partisan and issue opponents all give him high marks for being true to himself and his heritage.

Mike has time for friend and foe alike and seems to truly want to improve the lot of his constituents. When I spoke with him last week, he was already exploring the possibility of a mobile campaign office that would serve the far-flung corners of the largest CD east of the Mississippi River. This is, no doubt, the first of many good ideas and techniques he will bring to the second CD with its many problems and its collective loss of hope. A mill worker for 28 years, he knows what that means.

Mike Michaud's victory brings satisfaction and a sense of accomplishment to his campaign team and supporters. It also provides a powerful surge of pride in the whole statewide Franco American community. The Francos finally have a champion of their own.

Mike Michaud did what no other discernable Franco had ever been able to do and the political system of Maine is richer for his accomplishment.

Now the Franco American community is not simply in play.

Now it is leading the way! It's a grand moment in Maine political history.

II

THE DYNAMICS OF THE CAMPAIGN PROCESS

INTRODUCTION

To "Outsiders," those men and women who only see politics through the eyes of these reporters who cover politics and the 30 second commercials, politics can seem to be a blur of press releases and short stories on the nightly news. This is especially true today whereas twenty or thirty years ago, the print media covered campaigns much more closely and sent reporters out on the campaign trail to get a sense of why one campaign was winning or "coming on" and another was losing or "fading."

In this section, I have tried to capture the ebb and flow and above all the dynamics of campaign choices that one candidate makes versus another. The Yin and the Yang of politics requires interacting campaigns to make a set of decisions, some making the correct ones, others failing to take advantage of an opportunity or to limit the damage of a set back.

Also, recent elections in Maine saw a plethora of candidates, many of whom were drawn by the appeal of an open or almost open position. Almost all had high expectations when the contests began although one by one, including the survivors suffered reality checks along the way.

Capturing campaigns as they were disintegrating or emerging into contention is not easy to do but the essays which follow were written at the time of these critical turning points and remain far more poignant for their contemporary perspicuity. With hindsight, everything is clear but "in the moment" some trends are less clear than others!

Interested readers can see in the snapshots taken in mid-campaign how the races were shaping up at a particular moment in time even though many people where unaware of the internal dynamics of the campaigns in question. It is capturing those dynamics *in situ* which are the most challenging and the most rewarding.

After the election's outcome, many can see what went right and what went wrong and many will even profess to see a preordained outcome. But during the election itself, there are often wild mood swings on the part of the electorate, the press and even political insiders.

The meteoric rise and fall of the gubernatorial campaign of Judge Daniel Wathen is captured in two of the chapters in this section, chapters which literally and in the moment, capture the arc of that political skyrocket was going up and coming down. After it was all over, many professed to have seen it all coming; but at the time, the press, the sitting governor and his staff and many, many others saw it as the wave of the future.

REALITY CHECK

The season of dreams is almost over. Once the Legislature adjourns for the year, the many legislators and political want-to-be's will leave Augusta and will be left to their own devices. While the Legislature is in session, it is possible to dream the impossible dream, to think about running for higher office and to be stimulated by the mini-campaigns of others. Why not? Every other legislator is doing the same thing!

For candidates and would-be candidates, it has been quite easy to chat with friendly and conveniently placed reporters—who may want information as much a providing it—and to conjure up dreams of glory. Statements of wish fulfillment such as "I'm thinking about running for governor—or Congress—or the U.S. Senate" ramble around the Capitol in various crescendos. Anyone can be considering any run and still get a half decent response under the capitol dome. Few fellow legislators have said, "Boy, that's a bad idea, you'll get slaughtered."

But once the Legislative session is over, reality begins to kick in. The season of dreams comes to an end and the true demands of running for higher public office become apparent.

Over the years, I've noticed there are some reoccurring patterns that can be quite amusing as you watch them unfold. Here are a few to watch and, if you or someone you love is thinking about running for office above that of state senator, ponder.

First, sympathetic reporters, who listened and nodded while the session was in full bloom, now won't return phone calls, will refuse to print self-serving press releases and no longer have any inhibitions about mocking your candidacy. Once you are a "candidate" instead of a sitting legislator, your stock diminishes rapidly.

This is especially true if you have held a leadership position. Reporters who had to pay attention to your whims and opinions when you were an important source now lose interest in anything you have to say. This is very noticeable if you are say, Senate President. Just ask Duke Dutremble and Mark Lawrence how interested reporters were in their activities once the session was over and they were trying to make it to Congress or the U.S. Senate.

Having a leadership post in the Legislature guarantees reporters have to listen to you. Having *had* a leadership post in the Legislature guarantees reporters will pay you less attention when you become a candidate.

The second theme which I've seen occur over and over has to do with legislators and how they treat their colleagues in the State House.

Most candidates try to get their fellow legislators to sign on to their campaigns in order to show a breadth of support and how highly regarded they are by their peers. This is all to the good if the candidate wants only to make his or her letterhead look good. Legislators can perform that function quite well.

What candidates fail to realize is that fellow legislators sign on for a variety of reasons—they want your support for their bills, they know you are a powerful committee chair, they don't want to face you every day after having told you "no." So they are not always "supporting" you because they think you can—or should—win.

Moreover, once having signed on with one candidate, other candidates show great displeasure and to make up for it, legislators may sign on with other candidates as "secret supporters." I was once involved in a three way primary for governor and when the candidates got together after the election to exchange " secret supporter" lists, it was amusing to note that one prominent legislator was on all three "supporter" lists although the candidates all agreed that the legislator "hadn't really done much."

Fact is, most legislators don't do much work on other people's campaigns. Most legislators don't mind being on a letterhead or two or a list of secret supporters (or two), but as far as doing any real grass roots effort on behalf of the candidates, don't hold your breath. In thirty years of politics, I can count on one hand the number of situations where specific legislators actually worked hard enough to truly help elect a fellow legislator to higher office.

Often, if a particular legislator is perceived as being "on your side" she or he often will bend over backwards to be nice to the other candidates when they come to town, even taking them around with a startling exuberance just to make up for their earlier support of you.

Finally, the biggest change in campaign realities comes from the true size of the arena. It is one thing to have a "campaign" in Augusta and your home district. It is quite another to project that effort on a congressional district or the whole state. Paul Hazelton, one of the founders of the Muskie revolution of 1954 was fond of remarking that you couldn't appreciate retail politics in Maine if you didn't have a morning meeting in Calais, a noon meeting in Rumford and an evening meeting in Saco. So many legislators take the formula (such as door to door campaigning) that worked in their local district and try to project it onto a canvas that is far too broad and they end up frustrated and discouraged.

TIME SPEEDED UP BY EVENTS

While all political campaigns have their own rhythm and "feel," some are more distinctive than others. The 2002 Democratic congressional primary in Maine's second CD is shaping up to be a classic of timing and pace. Because of Congressman Baldacci's early decision to seek the Blaine House, and his own improbable rise during the 1994 cycle, many Democratic candidates are off and running 16 months before the general election. All believe they can win both the primary and the 2002 general election.

Part of this early activity is also due to campaign time being speeded up by events. Events trigger counter events and the timing of the entire campaign is set in motion prematurely. Candidate X begins earlier than usual, causing an earlier entry by Candidate Y. With more and more candidates chasing a relatively fixed pool of volunteers and money, a sense of urgency develops all across the board and candidates start earlier and earlier to do the things they ordinarily would wait until next year to attempt.

There are already five quite credible candidates and the political Spirit of Christmas Future allows each to dream of redemption and/or success. With over half of Democratic primary voters currently undecided about current candidates in my early soundings, all legitimately can produce in their own minds scenarios under which they emerge victorious.

What follows are my initial impressions of that race. These impressions are just that: highly personal, subjective and based on in fragmentary, initial polling data and interviews with party stalwarts but I believe they establish an early and rough hierarchy of the race.

One of the three current frontrunners is clearly Senate President Mike Michaud. He shows early signs of acquiring "muscle"—money, union organizers and savvy political advisors such as John Martin, Pat Eltman, Jim Mitchell and Phil Merrill. Current weaknesses: can seem a shy, almost diffident campaigner when outside his comfort zone, and some Democrats think his pro-Life position could be a handicap in the general election.

Currently also in the first tier is Kaileigh Tara, Lewiston's very popular mayor. Perhaps the best street campaigner in the contest, she exudes zest and campaign spirit and loves the thrill of political battle. She also has the most secure demographic base. She already shows surprising strength districtwide and could make good inroads in the St. John Valley. Current weaknesses: needs to raise enough money to expand on her LA base and get a coherent message package.

Susan Longley also starts out with some positive name identification not only from her coastal base, but also from her father and brother's previous runs. As a candidate, she can be very charming, even persuasive one on one. Very determined and a quick study. Current weaknesses: perceived by some to be mercurial and needs political allies in other parts of the state to build on the name identification.

These three are currently setting the pace.

Somewhat farther back in the early preliminary soundings is State Senator John Nutting. Hard working and likeable, he seems to be exactly the type of citizen-legislator envisioned by the framers of the Constitution ("Got to go home and milk the cows"). Current weaknesses: few political observers seem willing to say he can win. Will need more money to become competitive with Michaud on TV and needs an early break-out event or endorsement to become credible to many Democrats.

Also trailing in the early going is Sean Faircloth. Bright, supremely self-confident, and hard working, Faircloth has a very coherent and rational campaign strategy: "own" the Bangor-Old Town-Orono axis and finish second everywhere else. He got 25% of the vote statewide against Joe Brennan, capitalizing on Brennan's left wing weakness.

Faircloth's primary weakness seems to be a tendency toward overblown self-promotion: "I am the heir to FDR, Truman and J.F. Kennedy." Of course, all candidates—and political pundits (including myself)—have big egos but Faircloth seems truly special. He could probably double his voter appeal by toning down his rhetoric.

With Mary Cathcart and Dan Gwadowsky out of the race, the field is nearly decided although two candidates who have yet to decide about 2002 could offer Democrats even more choices.

Pat McGowan is one. He is the potential candidate many believe would give the Democrats the very best chance to hold the seat. Bright, hardworking and extremely likeable, he wears very well on the campaign trail. He is also the most experienced in districtwide general elections, having run two very credible races against a powerful incumbent, Olympia Snowe, losing the second time primarily because the Green candidate, Jonathan Carter, siphoned off 8.8% of the vote. Current weaknesses: all that good party water-carrying was nine years ago and primary voters have very, very short memories. He would need to establish his own primary credentials and raise more money than Michaud.

Finally, there is possible newcomer Lori Handrahan. She could have the potential to become the Henry Cabot Lodge of this campaign cycle, coming from an international and national vantage point to impact the local political scene. In my discussions with her, she has the clearest and most consistent message of reform. Although the second CD is a very hard arena in which to begin, her freshness might well strike a chord with voters who have not yet found their candidate.

For these latter candidates, as for all the others, however, time is truly speeded up by events. All must make their moves early this fall—if they are going to be competitive.

In politics, time is relative to the activities of others.

HERE COMES THE JUDGE

I have a confession to make.

I'm delighted to have former State Supreme Court Chief Justice Dan Wathen in the 2002 race for governor.

I say that even though I personally like John Baldacci a lot and almost went to the 2002 Senior Prom with him. I say that even though my son Erik's firm is doing the advertising for Peter Cianchette. I say that even though my wife and I personally have donated money to the John Jenkins for Governor campaign because we believe no matter who wins the race, Jenkins should be in it.

Why my delight?

I'm glad the Judge is running because I love time travel.

Ever since I was a kid, I have enjoyed science fiction, especially stories about time travel. The writings of Ray Bradbury, Poul Anderson and Brian Aldiss captured my imagination and held it. It's always exciting to go back in time and see the past come to light and experience a bygone age.

Now that's what Judge Wathen's campaign has brought me to date—a political time capsule. Thus far, he's provided us with a campaign right out of 1950. "No polling," he said at his announcement, "no consultants, no media firms." That's the way people campaigned in 1950. That's the way the political process worked so long ago. It's exciting to look back and see the way things were done 50 years ago. And I applaud him for bringing us, however momentarily, a glimpse of Christmas past.

And it certainly is working for The Judge. The sycophantic press corps troops up to his house in Augusta whenever he wants and writes down his every word. The *Portland Press Herald* recently ran two pictures of the little devil, one of which showed him indeed sitting on his porch as if it were 1950. Or 1850 for that matter. I love it!

But the problem with time travel is that it brings with it paradoxes and conundrums galore.

Now, I don't know precisely how the Judge is going to do in the political arena although some of my good political friends—John Christie, Alex Ray, George Smith and Mike Healey—believe he is just what this political season needs. George Smith, however, may have some problems with the Judge's chief fundraiser, Buzz Fitzgerald. Not only is Buzz a life long Democrat and placater of labor unions, but he's the head of something called "Citizens for Hand Gun Control." Odd bit of grizzle for the head of SAM to swallow.

Of course, I don't know where the Judge ultimately will end up. But this much I do know, unless the laws of political gravity have been suspended for this race, he's already made a huge mistake. His statement about doing this race without professional political assistance is an echo from the very distant past. In 1950, candidates, especially Republican candidates, didn't need pollsters, or consultants or media firms. All they needed to do was be themselves—successful Republican types. After all, in the decade of the 1940's, Republicans won every single governorship, Senate or House race that was up for grabs. Every single one.

In 2001, however, "No polling, no consultants, no media firm means something very different. In 2001, "No polling, no consultants, no media firm equals NO CHANCE."

Thus one of two things will happen. Judge Wathen will lose and lose ignominiously or he will change his viewpoint radically. He will alter his campaign strategy dramatically and he will hire a pollster and consultants and a media firm or he will lose.

You simply cannot campaign in the twenty-first century the way you did 50 years ago, even if the Maine press is incredibly sympathetic toward you. And I've never seen the Maine press corps so mesmerized by a political figure in 30 years of following politics. They worship this guy and give him passes on just about everything and the free publicity they've given him is more than they've given all the other candidates put together.

Part of the misperception about campaigns and how they are waged may be due to the illusion that the two Independent governors, Longley in 1974 and King in 1994, did it on their own. In fact, of course, without the brilliance of Jack Havey and Beryll Ann Johnson of Ad Media, Longley would not have made it to the Blaine House. And Angus King had one of the strongest campaign teams ever assembled in his 1994 venture.

You can't do it alone.

You can't do it with your wife's cell phone.

You can't just jump in to the political realm and wander around any old way you feel like.

Remember the incredibly enduring truth of the 1970's film with Robert Redford called "The Candidate." Robert Redford says he will be the candidate but "I want to go where I want and say what I want and do what I want." His astute campaign manager, speaking for all political professionals, writes his reply on the back of a matchbook. "You lose."

Folksy loners make good copy and can hold the press attention for a while, but ultimately, believing in that self-image is a fatal flaw.

Over time, the Judge is too smart to believe in his own image and will act accordingly. Look for the Judge to do a major flip-flop sooner rather than later. Look for the Judge to sign up a highly professional campaign team—with pollsters and consultants and media people—before the end of the year.

THERE GOES THE JUDGE

God this is fun!

No sooner was the ink dry on my last column when the Judge, Dan Wathen, candidate for the Republican nomination for governor, went out and hired the political consulting firm Savvy, Inc. led by Dennis Bailey and the polling firm of Critical Insights. I love predictions that come true!

But no sooner was the ink dry on *those* contracts when the Judge decided he'd had enough of politics and dropped out of the race. True to the off-handed way he entered the race, the Judge dropped out precipitously and somewhat gratuitously, leaving behind a wide range of supporters high and dry. Many were incredulous.

Apparently the Judge had not been sleeping well and had lost 25 pounds and didn't like the person he was becoming on the campaign trail as a "politician."

Fair enough, for the campaign trail isn't for everyone. In fact, I'd hate to have to do what the Judge and other candidates have to go through to get elected. I decided 30 years ago when I wanted to run for governor that while I love politics, I would hate being a candidate. So I have considerable sympathy for the Judge and those reasons for dropping out.

Unfortunately, the Judge didn't leave it there.

Now I don't fault him for not laying out another obvious reason he dropped out: his failure to arouse any significant interest on the part of those Republicans who would actually be voting in the primary.

But I do fault him for gratuitously holding up "politicians" as something he never wanted to be. That was a cheap shot and rang very false to me. By his own admission, nobody asked the Judge to become "a politician." He decided that all on his own. In fact, had he asked anybody they probably would have told him to run as an Independent and run as a so-called Clean Elections candidate so that he wouldn't have to ask ordinary people for cash, just belly up to the public trough and dive right in.

Mostly, however, I found the Judge's remarks about politicians very insulting. He sounded as if he had suddenly just found himself in a leper colony and wanted no part of them and feared whatever they had would rub off on him if he stayed! That was a very cheap shot. I have known hundreds of "politicians" in Maine and for the most part, they all deserve our thanks for taking time out from their daily lives to undergo the grueling and taxing political process.

The Judge was, as many who knew him agreed, intelligent and witty. I enjoyed meeting him at our Bowdoin candidate fair and shared a delightful luncheon with him. Out of the political arena, he seems like a classy guy. In it, he seemed totally at sea. But the truth of the matter is this: Maine is chock full of bright, witty, classy, public-spirited people. They don't all make good candidates.

Being a politician, especially running for a major office, takes a ton of effort, perseverance and a willingness to put in long, often thankless hours. Those who get off their duffs and out into the public arena and take their shots without whining and whimpering about how tough it is deserve our acclaim, not our approbation.

As for the press, the Judge apparently found them too harsh and demanding. All I can say about that is in thirty years of following politics in Maine, I've never seen the press corps so mesmerized by a candidacy. And so gentle to the candidate. Most of the working press treated the Judge with a deference they never accord others.

There is a real lesson here. Many of the working press conveyed to me their eagerness and excitement about the Judge. Many admitted that they had already assumed that Baldacci would be elected governor (no matter how the race will actually shape up ten months from now!) and that nothing short of some deus ex machine could stop his coronation. The Judge was their deus ex machine. What rubbish!

It's truly amazing that these supposedly knowledgeable guardians of the public information transmission belt would flock so readily to his unproven standard.

Normally so cynical about campaigns and candidates, they lined up to applaud this "pure" juggler from another milieu and welcomed him into the political center ring with such enthusiasm they simply added to the disrespect they already show to the existing serious candidates for governor. It is a travesty for political reporters to "decide" ten months or more in advance who is going to win a race and then proceed to help make that assumption come true by giving poor coverage to any and all challengers.

As for the "pure" juggler who dropped into the center ring for so few short moments, his is now a strange legacy. Ironically, Judge Wathen probably will not now be remembered for his fine service on the bench but for his bizarre dive into that political center ring and out of it again, all in a thrice.

Political insiders already have a term for the incident of the "pure" juggler. "To do a Wathen" now means to jump in and out of a race thoughtlessly and carelessly and to be unmindful of the people who flocked to ringside to help him improve his act.

It takes guts and drive and a true sense of inner worth to slog it out day by day with the voters. It takes humility to put up with reporters' self-fulfilling prophecies and distain for your press releases. It takes a tough inner core to put up with all the bullshit of politics. It's not for everybody. It's certainly not for elitists who expect to be elected by acclamation.

Give me an ordinary politician any day.

A SINKING SHIP?

Dave Flanagan's quest for the governorship was always a long shot, one predicated on many unlikely things happening. So the fact that his gubernatorial campaign ship has been taking on water lately and recently had his crew leap off to safety is not totally unexpected. Now, even a third place finish could be problematical.

It has never been clear what Flanagan was counting on to propel his craft to the Blaine House. There was early talk of the "Ice Storm" but wasn't it the crews from North Carolina who really carried the day? There was also a lot of emphasis on his Harvard credentials and being "the business candidate" at his website. But then Dana Connors of the Maine Chamber of Commerce and major power broker insisted that his name be taken off the website list of supporters, seriously undercutting Flanagan's claim to be the "business" candidate.

Flanagan may have also been counting on the endorsement of Governor King. Now I am not privy to whom the governor will endorse—if anyone—but I would put Flanagan's chances for that right up there with those of Mary Adams and Brownie Carson.

But all of this was before Flanagan's campaign staff quit.

I've never heard of any major candidate having all of his staff not only abandoning the campaign but also urging him to drop out because he didn't inspire them. If you can't inspire your own staff, how can you expect to inspire voters?

Hiring Dave Bustin—most recently bounced out as mayor of Hallowell—to set things right may seem like a strange move to some. Unless, as one Democratic wag put it to me, unless Flanagan is bound and determined to keep a firm hold on his ultimate base of support among those who dine at Slate's. Where is Frank O'Hara when we need him? It's all very curious.

I believe the political math just isn't there for Flanagan and hasn't been from the beginning. No matter how many old Brennanistas say "Run Davey Run" to bring Baldacci down to earth as payback for Baldacci's failure to put Joe over the top in the 1996 U.S. Senate race, victory doesn't seem very realistic.

Remember, for *any* Democrat turned Independent, there is only *one* path to the Blaine House that works and on that path, three things—with a total of five different variables—must be present. The only model that worked in the whole of the twentieth century requires *all* to be present for a Democrat turned Independent to win.

First and second, the Democrat/Independent must win major segments of two specific groups: urban Francos *and* rural Republicans. Third and fourth, *both* major parties must nominate candidates who are either poor candidates or who run poor campaigns. It is not enough that one major party candidate run poorly, both must. Fifth, there can only be a single credible Independent candidate. That formula is exactly how Longley won in 1974 and that is exactly how King won in 1994. Historically, there is no other way for a Democrat-turned-Independent to win.

This time, I don't think Flanagan can count on *any* of the five variables. Who can seriously see him appealing to urban Francos or rural, small town Republicans? Not after a lifetime of being a big government Democrat and a big business, quasi-monopoly Democrat. Plus, whether you like Baldacci or Cianchette for the winner of the governor's race, you can't expect that *both* major party candidates would run such lousy campaigns that Flanagan's would look good by comparison. And he isn't the only Independent running.

Faced with this configuration, I don't believe Flanagan can win the governorship and indeed must now do some very specific things in order to make it to a third place finish. The recent upheavals in his campaign and the very poor publicity they brought cast into sharp relief the distinct possibility that Flanagan may not finish third but fifth. I wouldn't be surprised if his own polls now show him no higher than 3–4% in any gubernatorial match-up.

But all is not yet lost. Dave Flanagan is tough minded, bright and tenacious. I believe Captain Dave can act vigorously and perhaps stop further drift downward. But Captain Dave must go below decks while there is still time and break out the cash. The serious cash. He needs to spend at least $1.5 million dollars of his own CMP buyout money to get in a position to sew up third place instead of the fifth place. Dave's campaign has been taking on considerable water. Only a lot of his cash stuffed in the holes can plug the leaks.

Making it to third place is no slam-dunk. Don't forget, this is the election when his two principle independent opponents, Jonathan Carter and John Jenkins each get $1 million of public funds just for showing up under the so-called Clean Elections Act and Jenkins in particular has an excellent positive to negative ratio in terms of public opinion. So unless he spends a ton of his own money, Flanagan could be outspent and outplaced by both Carter and Jenkins.

It is probably too early to project Flanagan to finish sixth behind newcomer Steve Kenney of Biddeford. But it is not too early to point out that Kenney, a financial consultant and president of the Maine Taxpayers Equity Alliance, will also have a cool $1 million. And Kenney went to the University of Maine, not Harvard.

THE IDES OF MARCH

In politics, March is often the cruelest month. The previous excitement of campaign beginnings and the positive appeal of a free slate, those moments when anything seems possible, have begun to fade. The cruel realities of funding, positioning and the lining up of supporters have begun to take their toll. In mid March, the primaries are still far enough away so there is not yet the sense of immediacy with its concomitant adrenalin rush of coming to the finish line.

As to final outcomes, much has yet to be determined. But much has already been determined. For some, like Bob Dunfey, the race is already over. And what a fiasco it was.

For other campaigns, there are critical days ahead and how they face the new realities will determine whether they will have an impact on the outcome. And for political insiders, there is considerable entertainment in these unfolding events during the ides of March.

For example: *The "Flanagan Follies" continue.* Although Dave Flanagan followed the good advice given in this column back in January by putting more of his own money into the campaign and hiring professionals such as Dennis Bailey of Savvy, Inc., his campaign continues to show signs of wear and tear.

No sooner had the next crew come on board, than Dave announced the names of 45 of his "supporters." Immediately, there was quite a hue and cry as a number of "supporters" turned out to be for other candidates. To the spirited notes first uttered by several wise troopers of the Seventh Cavalry, "Please Mister Custer, I don't want to go," they leapt off the Flanagan craft and tried to swim to dry land—or pointed to themselves already on dry land and claimed never to have gotten their feet wet on the now-awash decks.

Important power brokers such a Jon Doyle (Republican) and Douglas Carr (Democrat) seemed both amused and embarrassed by the Flanagan listings, although one Democratic power lady, Janet Mills, was not. Mills, who was thought to be interested in the Attorney General's position, came out squarely for Flanagan, certainly a courageous—if odd strategy—for someone needing Democratic votes to become AG.

The formation of the "The Unholy Alliance" amused many. Who would ever have thought it possible? Mike Heath, Paul Volle and John Hathaway united around the theme of "family values." Mike Heath, frustrated in his unchristian mission to take away health benefits from the significant others of gays and lesbians, suddenly and belatedly found a champion for "family values" in the unlikely figure of John Hathaway.

Hathaway, who has been dogged for years about an alleged incident with a young babysitter, was undoubtedly relieved to hear that Heath had pronounced the alleged incident only "a last minute smear tactic" and not a matter of moral concern.

Heath, already famous for his odd distinction between sin and sinner, did a huge back flip and abandoned Jim Libby, the family values chap previously claiming his affection, stating Libby wasn't vocal enough. Truth be told, I think Libby was too vocal, constantly bleating in the media that he was having a hard time getting signatures. It's hard to be a winner when you're always whining.

For his part, Hathaway continued to maintain that the alleged incident in question never happened. Knowing the fearsome tenacity of the Maine press corps, however, he then cleverly promised a press conference to clear the air about the incident and then went blithely off, never giving it. The press mavens, led by such stalwarts as Paul Carrier, Joshua Weinstein, Fran Quinn and Glenn Adams let him get away with this skillful tactic. My hat's off to Hathaway for correctly anticipating their reactions, or lack thereof.

These chaps, who had so fervently rushed off to cover Dan Wathen's announcement that he was going bird hunting like it was the Second Coming, now shied away from any serious investigative reporting or even a rudimentary effort to hold Hathaway accountable for his promise to hold the press conference in order to clear the air! John Day and Steve Campbell truly left a hole in Maine journalism we only dimly perceived at the time of their departure from the scene.

In addition, Hathaway, claiming to be the "true conservative," announced that he was racing to the government's trough to get public financing! This is like something out of Alice in Wonderland, watching "true conservative" candidates like Libby and Hathaway claim that personal raids on the state treasury for political funds are truly "conservative" in nature. What an amusing spectacle.

Then there was the strange, surrealistic campaign of Bob Dunfey. After signing up one of the strongest campaign teams in the current field, Dunfey went on to raise hardly any money and been strangely diffident on the campaign trail. Despite a great campaign team led by Josh Boisvert, Dunfey ran one of the most epigonic major campaigns in modern times, refusing to criticize his primary opponent—about anything—and unwilling to put the financial resources behind his campaign in order to make it credible. Right up until the end, he continued to act as if Chellie Pingree were running for some other nomination other than the one he is seeking!

Under considerable pressure from Democrats in Maine and Washington, he dropped out before the ides of March, denying Chellie Pingree the chance to beat a ghost.

His bizarre campaign style aside, insiders continue to ask, why did Dunfey get into a race against Chellie Pingree once she'd been finessed out of the governor's race by John Baldacci if Dunfey wasn't going to run a serious campaign? I'll bet Joe Brennan would like to know the answer.

The ides of March are upon us.

UZI SUZIE

Not too long ago, I received a breathless, excited late night phone call from a prominent Democratic activist. "Uzi's going down, Uzi's going down," he exclaimed, referring to Maine's junior senator in the argot of the Democratic left. I think Susan Collins got her "Uzi Suzie" nickname for her strong support of Maine hunting and fishing community and her previous endorsements from the powerful Sportsman's Alliance of Maine but "Uzi Suzie" she remains to some in the Democratic Party.

I was truly surprised at this assumption of vulnerability since in my polling Senator Collins has generally been among Maine's most popular figures, with positive ratings well over 70% and negatives in the low teens. Within six or nine months of going to Washington, Collins has been right up there with Snowe and King in terms of favorability.

"Why would you think she's vulnerable?" I asked, assuming that legitimate Democratic polling had her just as strong as I. Otherwise, I thought, how to explain Tom Allen standing recently on the podium with Chellie Pingree, endorsing her for the U.S. Senate when only a week before she was running for governor?

Surely, I thought, if Collins were the least bit vulnerable, Allen would not have been sharing the podium with Chellie and John Baldacci but with George Mitchell and the shade of Ed Muskie.

Of course the supreme irony for Allen continues: if those urging Governor King to seek the first District congressional seat prevail next fall, Allen's "safe" seat will be his "jeopardized" seat. But more of this later.

"No polling, but Porter says she's vulnerable," replied the activist to my question. Oh my goodness, what an insider's insider moment I thought! Here was a prominent and usually astute Democratic activist about to make a political commitment not based on polling or common sense but simply responding to a column by the liberal-almost-to-the point-of-caricature, John Porter of the *Portland Press Herald/Maine Sunday Telegram.*

And what a column it turned out to be when I finally got to read it. Porter's claim of Collins' "vulnerability" was based in part on her "go along" attitude toward George W. Bush and his budget and because she had—get this "sin"—voted to let the President of her party have his choice for Attorney General! Porter then went on to denigrate Collins' "retail" political skills. I idly wondered when was the last time Porter had been north of Augusta, let alone out on the campaign trail with Collins who, in my not so humble opinion, is outstanding in small groups.

The point here, however, is not to mock a bizarre, even silly column. Rather, when I heard the mindset of "Uzi's" vulnerability, I immediately thought of 1960. In that year, the Democrats, faced with an extremely strong Margaret Chase Smith, thought that the way to beat the appeal of one woman was to run another one against her.

This reverse feminism, truly worthy of the hypocrisy of Emily's List, produced a match-up of two women, one with national as well as state credentials and the other with state legislature experience. Déjà vu!

The only problem with the scenario in 1960 was that Margaret Chase Smith was perfectly positioned in the middle of the political spectrum. Feisty and independent, she got few invitations to the White House but appealed to the broad segments of Maine society. A Republican, she nevertheless cared deeply about working men and women and her support from the blue collar Franco American communities was high enough so that no Democratic challenger could come close to her coalition of rural Republicans and urban Francos.

She buried Cormier 62% to 38%.

Collins too seems ideally suited for the present Maine political culture. She is strong on national defense, small business, a balanced budget and free trade, but she is also pro choice and has an extremely positive stance on consumer issues and the environment. Her voting record on the sensitive issue of the environment alone is going to make it very hard for her to be attacked with credibility. Members of the Appalachian Mountain Club, National Fish and Wildlife Federation, Audubon Society, Sierra Club, Friends of the Earth, Natural Resources Council of Maine and Environmental Defense, and The Nature Conservancy will all have to be persuaded that her strong record should count for nothing if they are to endorse her opponent.

On the issues that matter the most to Maine people, she is very well positioned in the middle of the political spectrum. She will be very hard to dislodge by legitimate means.

What Porter and others of the extreme liberal portion of the political spectrum forget—and their error is duplicated by the far right in Maine politics who are currently muttering that Collins and Snowe aren't "loyal" enough to Bush—is that in Maine politics, the center holds.

Only rarely and in extraordinary circumstances do left wing or right wing candidates win. Pingree can try to move dramatically to occupy the middle, as did Tom Andrews against Olympia Snowe in 1994, but to get away with such a major re-positioning and re-packaging move, the Collins campaign people will truly have to be asleep at the switch.

Of course, Democratic insiders have yet to muscle Bob Dunfey out of the primary race as they recently did Chris Harte (with a good deal of lingering bitterness no doubt) but no matter.

Look for "Uzi Suzie" to gun down the competition in the fall of 2002, whether that competition turns out to be male or female.

Postscript: In November, 2002, Collins swamped Pingree 58% to 42%, echoing the previous victory of her hero, Margaret Chase Smith over another Democratic woman, Lucia Cormier in 1960.

ELECTIONS AND THE ROLE OF BIOGRAPHY

It is difficult, if not impossible, to understand the progress of the major elections of the 2002 cycle without a fundamental appreciation of the role biographical commercials (or "bio ads") play in many political races.

There is a truism among most political insiders that when a candidate is challenging an incumbent or a much better known political figure, he or she must establish an identity *before* they can start attacking their opponent. The reason for this seems to be that if people don't know anything about you, and you start by attacking your opponent, they end up associating you with the negative attacks. But if the voting public has some biographical information first and gets to know you, then they accept subsequent negative attacks on your opponents much better.

Surprisingly, many major candidates and their campaigns ignore this basic bedrock principle. Chellie Pingree's campaign, for example, jumped into the U.S. Senate electronic wars last spring with a series of massive attacks on Collins over the question of prescription drugs. A half million dollars of TV time later, her competitive position hadn't improved at all and her own negatives had gone from 6% to 24%. Her image in her own commercials was harsh, querulous and seemingly mean spirited. She never even smiled.

All the while this was going on, the Collins campaign was able to spin out warm and fuzzy images of her helping everyone in Maine, from small business people to veterans to senior citizens. Only in mid October did Pingree come up with a bio ad which showed her grinning wildly—and continuously—as various citizens of North Haven weighed in on what a wonderful and caring person she was. A good ad, even a great ad, but one which should have been shown in April, not October before the numbers had hardened 2–1 in Collin's favor.

In much the same fashion, Jonathan Carter has completely squandered any chance he might have had to make the quest for the governorship a three-person race. Despite tons of advice to the contrary, he has never run his own biographical ad to set the stage for his candidacy. His previous thrashing around on forestry and other issues had resulted in a positive to negative ratio of 1 positive to 2 negative (compared with Baldacci's and Cianchette's 3–1 positive). And this, of course, was before the public got a chance to see Ken Swope's "Soprano" brand of humor—and many really, really disliked the fake-sounding Italian accents from New Jersey!

When you are running as a cause person and only interested in getting 5% of the vote, and have little or no money, you can ignore the biography dictum. But when you are seriously running for governor, need 25% of the vote to get competitive and have almost $ 1 million to spend, you cannot.

The odd thing is I believe Carter could be quite an attractive candidate. He has an engaging personality, fine sense of humor and an appealing story to tell about himself. He should have begun his serious campaign this summer by telling that story: who he is, where he came from and what shaped his values. He would be over 20% by now if he had.

Instead, Carter squandered much of his money beating the drums that he was the only so-called "Clean Elections" candidate and told viewers that their tax dollars were paying for his commercials. Now Maine people may have voted for "Clean Elections" but the vast majority had—at least until Carter told them—no idea it was their tax dollars that were paying for it. Many find that a very, very poor idea.

So, Carter has been hit with a triple whammy of his own making. First, he didn't bother to introduce himself with a biography ad. Second, he compounded this mistake by introducing himself with an issue nobody but ardent political insiders care much about (and they are deeply divided about it!). Then, he compounded *that* mistake by associating himself with something a huge number of Maine people oppose, namely using their tax dollars for political campaigns.

Not surprisingly, far from reducing his negatives, Carter's own commercials have driven them up and placed an artificial ceiling on his ultimate performance on election day. As we approach the end of October, he is limping along with about 10% of the vote and higher negatives then when he started!

Biography is turning out to be central to the second CD race as well, but in a very different way. Both candidates have seen its importance and made it central to their campaigns.

As my wife is fond of saying, I have a weak spot for blue collar candidates but I think Mike Michaud's story is one of America's finest: mill worker with high school education rises to top of Maine politics and becomes president of the senate and now wants to go to Washington. I found this a very appealing portrait and I thought he would have that base all to himself.

But the Raye campaign, first in the primary, and now in the general election, has refused to concede the upwardly mobile biographical territory to Michaud. With his former lineman father and various brothers telling Raye's rise through hard work story electronically, he has become very competitive as the campaign developed this fall.

That race can still go either way because the basic biographies of the candidates involved are both very appealing. All the negative advertising by the state and national political parties can't detract from the basic "story" of each candidate.

Campaign biographies thus remain a crucial ingredient to electoral success in Maine and those candidates who have ignored or badly played that element will lose in 2002.

III

THE DYNAMICS OF PUBLIC REFERENDA

INTRODUCTION

To me, there is something wonderful, exciting and even magical about ballot measures, the way the people can make public policy in Maine without—or in spite of—their elected representatives in the Legislature. Having citizens able to set public policy on their own goes to the heart of democracy.

In Maine over the last few decades, ballot measures have grown and grown in terms of their impact on public policy. This was not always the case. Mainers took for themselves the right to have citizen initiatives as well as Legislative offerings in 1908, during a surge of populist activity all across the United States. Maine ended up as one of the 22 states allowing for citizen-initiated ballot measures. But the process was used sparingly for the first half of the twentieth century.

In fact, referenda did not really play a major and sustained role in the political life of Maine until the 1980 referendum to shut down the Maine Yankee nuclear plant. This referendum attracted national attention, political operatives and funding and cast in sharp relief the referendum process for all to see.

The Maine Yankee issue not only spawned two more referenda on nuclear power, but set in motion a process whereby many groups and even individuals saw the referendum process as a way to bypass or overturn Legislative action. The result was a dramatic increase in the number of referenda on the Maine ballot.

For example, from 1960 until 1980 there were only a half-dozen citizen generated referenda, while from 1980 to 2004 there were over 30. Today it is a very rare election cycle in which there is not at least one, and more likely several, ballot measures to be decided on in June or November, even on "off year" elections.

In the recent past, Maine citizens decided on the possibility of Sunday sales in large stores, the income tax, shutting down Maine Yankee (3 times!), physician assisted suicide, timber cutting rules (3 times!), Gay Rights (3 times!), the widening of the Maine Turnpike (2 times), property tax relief (3 times!) along with many other environmental, land use and public policy issues.

In Maine, it is relatively easy to get a citizen's initiative on the ballot. Based on a percentage of the previous general election, state law requires only plus or minus 50,000 signatures of registered voters. This is an amount which can be relatively easily collected in a single election day. There is thus an acceptable avenue for interested national as well as local groups to get their issues before the people of the state without requiring the Legislature to initiative such action.

At the same time, the Legislature often uses the referendum process to avoid having to vote on highly contentious issues and the Legislature as well as citizens can send a proposal out to the voters.

Ballot measures also serve as safety valves for the political system. Citizen discontent can be channeled into politically useful rather than destructive ways, bringing them closer to their government and at the same time, able to show that they are ultimately the repository of political power.

VOX POPULI

"The Voice of the People." "Let the people speak" goes the common saying. At the same time, it is always good to know what the people are going to say before you ask them publicly.

I have always prided myself in taking the "worst case scenario" approach to any political polling. What is the most negative reading of a situation? What can and what should the client expect if she or he proceeds in one direction rather than another? What is the downside of this or that strategy? Which authority figure helps your cause and which hurts it and who makes no difference at all?

Over the years, clients have often told me that they prize this approach. Just because I—or they—want something to happen doesn't mean that the chances are likely it will, because as Ward Just puts it, "Expectation is the enemy of prediction."

I believe this is one of the reasons I was approached last summer by Representative Donald Soctomah, and other leaders of the Passamaquoddy tribe to vigorously test the possibility of bringing a gaming facility to their tribal land in Washington County.

Although I wholeheartedly supported—and continue to support—that concept, I told them I would only advise them and poll for them if I could ask the toughest questions. To their credit, they only wanted the hardest and most realistic look at their situation.

To try to shed some light on the current debate—and with Representative Soctomah's permission—let me show you what we find when we ask various questions about Indian gaming and you can be the judge as to the relevance of any of our findings for the upcoming debate.

The Passamaquoddies tested the concept of bringing a gaming facility to Maine in the following way:

1. We stated that the gaming facility would be on Indian land;
2. That the gaming facility would only be in Washington County;
3. That the gaming facility had to have the approval of the residents of Washington County as well as the whole state;
4. That all four of Maine's Indian tribes, the Passamaquoddies, the Penobscots, the Micmacs and the Maliseets, would all share in the proceeds;
5. And that some of the proceeds would also be earmarked for state of Maine use, such as a percentage for the cost of prescription drugs for Maine's elderly poor.

In other words, we tested a very specific project located in a very specific area with local approval required. We also asked 600 Maine people, a sample 50% larger than most statewide surveys you see in the press. The Passamaquoddies wanted to be very accurate and this sample size got us a margin of error of plus or minus .038 at the 95th level of confidence.

As a result of this survey, the Passamaquoddies have the most accurate data of anyone on this particular project proposal.

The findings couldn't be clearer: the people of Maine strongly support the concept of an Indian gaming facility in Washington County.

They do so by a margin of more than 3–1!

Among all voters, the margin is 65% to 19%.

Among most likely voters, the 40% who will definitely show up no matter when the election is held, the ratio is 68% to 21%.

This proposal has the approval, not just of the people of Washington County but of every other county in Maine. Many like the idea of Canadians coming to Maine to spend their money on a gaming facility where the unemployment is over 11%. Many like the idea of the Native Americans having the opportunity to improve their own lives and take charge of their future.

Even among the largest tribes of Maine, there is widespread support. 71% of the Irish tribe and 70% of the Franco American tribe like it. Of course there is a slight fall down among the Governor King's own Anglo-Scottish tribe. Only 65% of them like it.

But that, as they say, "ain't all bad."

What is also interesting to me in the results was the high percentage of conservatives who like the idea of a gaming facility on native American land as a way to get the residents of Washington county "off welfare and onto the tax rolls" and the high percentage of liberals who like the idea of helping the native Americans put their lives back together. This is one issue where the ends of the political spectrum bend around and come together.

I have nothing but admiration for Donald Soctomah, Richard Stevens and the other Passamaquoddies who have already worked so hard to make this dream come true and who were so generous in wanting to share the positive employment and transportation aspects with their people, their Native American brothers, the people of Washington County and everyone in the state of Maine.

It would be a tragedy if this wonderful proposal got lost in the din over a proposed casino in Kittery, Maine, a location where to the best of my knowledge there are no Native Americans and where there is very low unemployment.

Postscript: The voters in Maine decided that while they liked a possible Indian gaming facility on Indian tribal land in Washington County where there was a lot of unemployment and a lot of Indians, they did not like the idea of an Indian casino in the heart of York County where there was very little unemployment and very few Indians. Over 70% voted NO on that alternative.

BEHOLD THE PSYCHOGRAPHICS

This fall's ballot measures reflect the increasing importance and use of psychographics in Maine political campaigns. Originally used in advertising and marketing to denote life style and consumer preferences, psychographics have become a valuable and useful tool in understanding Maine politics.

"Psychographic" refers primarily to the psychic imagery around which voters make decisions. It is a shorthand way of describing the "inner landscape" of the voters of Maine, the images they hold in their heads as they make public policy decisions. The use of psychographics turns out to be a highly valuable concept in determining why voters vote a certain way on certain issues at certain times and then vote another way at other times.

Part of this has to do with the basic and existing mind set of the voters; that is, what imagery they bring to a particular referendum or issue? And part of it has to do with the ability of various campaigns to reinforce, change or obliterate the existing imagery, by substituting new images and new connotations to older cognitive maps.

For example, in the 1991 referendum to stop the widening of the Maine Turnpike, opponents of the turnpike were highly successful in the run up to the election by providing powerful word pictures of wetlands. These "sacred wetlands," as they became known, and the wonderful ecosystems they contained were actually the drainage ditches to the side of the proposed wider highway.

Even though the "wetlands deficit" (which was to be offset with other created wetlands elsewhere), the power and majesty of the "sacred wetlands" concept overrode more pedestrian notions of what was at stake with many people. The upscale voters in the Portland suburbs, for example, voted against the widening in large part because of the environmental concerns.

In 1996, however, when the issue was reintroduced, the proponents of the widening superimposed another, more powerful image onto the sacred wetlands. This was the notion of traffic jams and the danger to one and all. Powerful and evocative commercials showing emergency workers trapped in traffic on the Maine Turnpike convinced voters that safety and emergency access were more important than worrying about the drainage ditches. The fact that so many of the upscale voters who had voted against the widening in 1991 had been stuck in traffic on their way to Boston in the intervening years didn't hurt either.

Or take the example of forest practices issues. Here I have traced two archetypes over the past twenty years. The first is one of "The Wild Wild East," with images of wilderness and forests where hunting and fishing is in a grand tradition and the scenery is magnificent, and trees are tall and cut, if at all, individually. The second is that of "The Industrial Forest" best captured by a Wilderness Society film featuring a gigantic, large-house sized machine coming through the woods, not only cutting every tree but literally picking them up by the trunks and shaking out the dirt from the roots.

The various debates over clear cutting have taken place within the context of these two images. Psychographically, people tend to vote based on the archetype they start with and retain or which can be placed or superimposed onto in their initial image. The Forest Compact went down to defeat primarily because of the powerful imagery used at the end by opponents of the Compact who featured industrial grade spraying threatening life and limb, children and grandchildren.

Conversely, in the forestry referendum of 2002, the carefully and lovingly tended plots of the small woodlot owners evoked a more positive and nostalgic look at the Great Maine Woods while the threat of sprawl was juxtaposed with a ban on clear cutting which might have led to more cutting (since a landowner had to cut 20% of his or her trees every year or lose the right to cut them). For the record, the Industrial Forest psychographic prevailed in the first two forestry referenda, while the Wild Wild East image took the third.

The competing life style and choices inherent in one's inner world views are also at the heart of the two current major debates. Take the proposed Indian casino in Sanford. Do you have an image of Maine which precludes such a facility? Do you feel that the LL Bean outdoor, Wild, Wild (but slightly tamed) East image is at odds with a possible gambling facility of that size, magnitude and advertising scope? Or do you have an inner landscape holistic enough to include a Maine of casinos and a Maine of LL Bean? Either image will help you make up your mind on the referendum this fall.

In the tax reform and school funding measures, psychographic markers are also at work. For the 1A supporters, their inner landscapes provide a call for local control, a belief that the elected officials in small towns and cities know what is best for their citizens, better than the Legislature and bureaucrats in Augusta and will, given a chance, improve education and reduce property taxes. For the 1B supporters, this inner landscape is perceived as chaotic and dominated by "the mob" and it must be countered by a dominant central authority model which uses "planning" and "projection" and "statistics" and extra-state models to subdue those who advocate local control.

In November, it will be interesting to see which inner landscapes cast the more powerful gravitational pull on the electorate. One thing seems certain, as the twenty-first century proceeds and there are more ballot measures and more public policy decisions decided each election cycle, the role of psychographics can only increase.

Individuals, groups, parties and corporations will only ignore these important aspects at their peril. These interior landscapes, these cognitive maps, give texture and meaning to the state's political and demographic dimensions.

SOME WHO MATTERED

Readers of my previous books will, I hope, remember the emphasis I often put on the nature of political campaigns themselves in determining outcomes. These campaigns qua campaigns, and the people who drive them to conclusion, are often overlooked in the swirl of contemporary news and analysis.

This year's smashing, amazing upset victory of Casinos No! is a classic case in point. Without specific individuals and their contributions, Casinos No! would not have succeeded. To illustrate this point, I have selected a sample of "some who mattered" to show those who made a difference in the political outcome of this critical election of 2003. There were many others, of course, and my apologies to those not mentioned due to the limitations of space. Nor does this order of mention denote a fixed hierarchy of value:

1. If you are glad no casino resort is coming to Sanford this year, there are none who more deserve your praise and credit than Lisa and Leon Gorman. Without their leadership, financial support and relentless pursuit of victory, Casinos No! would have fought a brave but losing fight. They showed a commitment to this state and its people virtually unparalled in my thirty years Maine experience. The people of Maine owe them an enormous debt of gratitude as the psychographic world of LL Bean ended up crushing the world of Las Vegas.

2. Toward this end, John Oliver, head of LL Bean's governmental affairs department, was the sine qua non of the campaign, expertly linking the many strands of the campaign, executing its various decisions and providing very perspicacious insights and managerial expertise.

3. Dennis Bailey, who for several years has battled casinos in all forms, fought a guerrilla war with skill and dispatch until there were enough troops and tanks and aircraft to carry the fight to the opponents' heartland. With humor and true political expertise, Dennis fought the hard, grinding day-to-day battle from beginning to end with whatever he had available in any given situation. He truly was the campaign core and assembled the entire team that ultimately won the day.

4. Greg Stevens, Erik Potholm and their creative and production crew at Stevens, Reed, Curcio and Potholm developed the TV and radio commercials that won the "shock and awe" phase of the air war with vivid and powerful imagery. Their contributions are now the stuff of legend. For her part, Janet Wyper should receive residual kudos into the indefinite future. What a screen presence! Also, Dave Emery's tracking was absolutely superb and constantly right on target.

5. Governor John Baldacci and former Governor Angus King get high marks as well. King came down out of the stands and onto the playing field after a six-year referendum absence to deliver "the cruel and Independent yuppies." Baldacci, in one of the most notable acts of political courage of this era, took on the blue collar base of his own party as well as that of the AFL-CIO, and helped to deliver much of the critical Franco American vote statewide. He proved once again to be an outstanding leader.

6. There were obviously many other political figures who fought the casino on many levels but none with more telling impact and élan than two Democratic senators, Janet Mills and Ethan Strimling. Mills, whose TV commercial changed 40,000 votes early in the fall, and Strimling, who showed his mettle in leading, not following, his Democratic base, look to have significant statewide roles in the future.

7. In this regard, no one showed more courage and mental toughness than the Warrior Princess, Val Landry. Facing ongoing harassment, verbal abuse and attempted intimidation, she soldiered on with verve and dispatch and incredible moral fiber, never losing her sense of purpose or humor. She was very impressive on many levels and in many venues.

8. Edith Smith Leary was the campaign manager in a most difficult situation, trying to juggle the interests and advice of many, many high-pow-

ered players. Her ability to get such diverse political figures as Mike Heath and Jonathan Carter to stick to an overall game plan was a major achievement. And accolades must also go to both Heath and Carter who put their personal agendas aside to serve the common good.

9. The Casino No! field staff and volunteers, led by Corey Hascall, made a huge difference particularly in southern Maine, turning out truly amazing margins in York and Cumberland counties and actually winning the GOTV fight in Sanford. Jeremy Payne, John Hessessy, Sara Yates, Jed Rathband, Chaz Cirame, Will Gardiner, Representative Mary Black Andrews and many others outfought the million-dollar ground game of their opponents with skill and dispatch. It was the best get out the vote effort I have witnessed in a long time.

10. The entire executive committee was also vital. Often, such committees are simply rubber stamps of the campaign professionals, but this one was different. Phil Harriman, Dave Flanagan, Chris Harte, George Isaacson, Durward Parkinson, Dave Nickerson, Tim Hussey, Jim Bartlett and others contributed vast amounts of time, energy, money and leadership as well as vital political savvy to make the campaign one of unusual substance and depth. George Campbell continues to be one of the state's most important, endearing and enduring operatives.

Moe Bisson did a truly outstanding job keeping the financial books and making sure the campaign spent its money wisely and in timely fashion. He deserves special praise as do the Verrill Dana team of Jamie Kilbreth and Valerie Wright who grounded the entire campaign in impeccable legal advice and solid factual underpinnings.

The 2003 battle over the proposed casino in Sanford was one of those watershed contests which shape the history and destiny of the Pine Tree State. Those women and men who battled so hard and long and skillfully must inevitably bring to mind an echo of the sentiments—if not the pronouns—of Shakespeare in *Henry V*:

> "And gentlemen in England now abed
> Shall think themselves accursed they were not here, and
> Hold their manhood cheap whiles any speaks
> That fought with us upon Saint Crispin's Day."

EVERYBODY WON?

The state of Maine owes the Maine Municipal Association and the Maine Education Association an enormous debt of gratitude for sponsoring the recent campaign for property tax relief and property tax reform. After 18 years of inaction by the Legislature and its steadfast refusal to do anything about Maine's over-reliance on the property tax to fund state services (46% versus most other states' 33%), there was a definite need to make this public policy problem front and center.

The MMA and MEA, working together, formulated 1A, a holistic, reformist, very fair and balanced plan to force the Legislature to meet its longstanding promise of funding 55% of the cost of K through 12 education (compared to the 42% the state currently provides). The passage of 1A could have resulted in property tax cuts of 15% in those communities which chose to use the new revenues for that purpose.

Governor Baldacci and some Legislative leaders, concerned over the timing and immediate nature of 1A, countered with another proposal (1B) which would fund approximately 50% of all education and 55% of so-called "core" education costs but would not achieve this goal for six or seven years.

But still other Legislative leaders, mostly Republican, insisted that both 1A and 1B were too expensive and ill timed and urged defeat of both measure. Proponents of 1C made much of the fact that they too favored property tax relief but wanted the opportunity for the Legislature to "do it right."

The result was a healthy, upbeat policy dust-up with vigorous campaigns run by all three groups. The 1A forces were effectively and courageously led by Chris Lockwood for the MMA and Rob Walker, Mark Gray and Steve Crouse for the MEA. The 1A citizens group was spearheaded by outstanding tri-captains Dana Lee, Nick Mavodones, Jennifer Wixson and the able president of the MMA, Sue Lessard. She in turn was supported by the fine executive committee of Ryan Pelletier, Galen Larrabee, Oz Bonsey and John Bibber. Geoff Herman, Mike Starn, Jeff Nevins, Kate Dufour, Laura Veilleux, Theresa Chavarie, Denise Kolreg, Krystal Ashe O'Sullivan and Chuck Jackson did yeoman service as well. They took the message of tax reform to all corners of the state.

For their part, the 1B forces were well led by Dana Connors of the Maine Chamber of Commerce, Kay Rand, Larry Benoit, Pat Eltman, Sue Bell and, after one of the most expensive breakfasts in the history of Maine politics, they were joined by many of Maine's business and production leaders herded by John Delahanty. 1B was also helped enormously by the active and ongoing engagement of the Governor. In fact, 1A was poised to achieve the necessary 50.1% of the vote until the very last week of the campaign when a strong TV commercial and appeal by Governor Baldacci, boosted 1B from a distant third place to a close second. The Governor's intervention was timely and decisive.

So 1A won the three way race with 38%, but supporters of 1B could justly claim they had won as well, since their vigorous campaign and vote total of 35% prevented 1A from getting 50%, and the 1C proponents, led by Bob Stone, could—and did—a argue that their 27% cost both 1A and 1B the chance to break 50%.

In November, 2003, everybody won.

But here's what is so interesting: if one takes 1A and 1B's total votes, it is clear that over 7 out of 10 Maine voters (73%) want property tax relief and property tax reform so the campaigns of both really underscored the deep-seated concern throughout the state for the unbalanced reliance on the property tax. Seventy percent of Maine people rarely agree on anything, but here they voted in record numbers for property tax relief and property tax reform. So all those voters who favor property tax relief won and won an overwhelming mandate for change.

Where will that change come from? To his considerable credit and ongoing leadership, Governor Baldacci wasted no time in reaching out to the 1A proponents, and even as this is written, proponents of 1A, 1B and even some from 1C are working on a "grand compromise" which could give the taxpayers of Maine much needed relief and a just reward for the voting patterns which showed such a strong majority of Maine voters in favor of property tax relief and reform. It will be a tough challenge in this year's economy but it is achievable with goodwill and a willingness to truly compromise and think outside the box on the part of all parties.

Will the Legislature go along with "a grand compromise" or even help craft one? One hopes so. Proponents of 1C argued that only the Legislature could solve the delicate and tricky issues of property tax reform. Now is their chance to weigh in with positive recommendations. It remains to be seen whether that was simply campaign rhetoric or a genuine statement of principle and purpose. Only if the Legislature rises to the occasion and gets serious about meaningful property tax reform and relief will the 73% of Maine voters have truly won. Does the Maine Legislature have the guts and vision to tackle this much-needed reform in an election year?

We would all like to think so, but we will all have to be shown that our citizen Legislature is truly up to the task. During the fall campaign, the Legislative leaders were adamant that they wanted a chance to fix the out-of-whack property system.

Now they have it.

Postscript: As unbelievable as it may seem, the Maine Legislature did nothing during its next session. That's right, nothing. The Legislature was unable to come up with any kind of alternative, compromise or meaningful attempt to reduce property taxes, adjourning on April 30, 2004 having failed to do anything about property tax relief. This ranks as one of the great failures of Maine's citizen legislature in modern times.

Carol Palesky, the head of a movement to cap property taxes at 1% of evaluation called it "disgusting." She was not far off the mark and one could only think of William Morris and his prophetic words from The Ballad of John Ball: "Men fight and lost the battle and the thing they fought for comes about in spite of their defeat, and when it comes, turns out not to be what they meant and other men have to fight for what they meant under another name." Forgive the gender incorrectness if you will, for William Morris knew of what he spoke.

On June 15, the voters of Maine, disturbed over the Legislature's failure to do anything regarding property tax relief voted 55% to 45% for the original 1A proposal!

"FREE MARTHA"

It was wild and wooly, totally exciting and off the charts, unlike any other election day I have ever experienced. March 9 was the day the little coastal community of Harpswell voted on project "Fairwinds," the proposed Liquefied Natural Gas (LNG) terminal for the abandoned U.S. Navy fuel depot.

Neither the pros nor the cons of the proposed LNG facility may have much relevance for readers of the Sun Journal, but the election day itself offers some highly amusing and interesting dimensions for all who live in a democracy to ponder.

Election Day, March 9, 2004 had many of the aspects of an election in Haiti or even Afghanistan. Supporters and opponents had both charged widespread intimidation and there were rumors voters would have to run a gauntlet of angry partisans. Taking no chances, the Cumberland County Sheriff's Department blanketed the area and surrounding roads with a massive police presence. I counted seven deputies at the one polling place open in town, plus a mobile command center. And that was *before* the bomb threat!

That's right, a bomb threat soon came through, claiming someone was going to blow up the school where the voting was being held, the Harpswell town hall and even the bridge connecting the two peninsulas of the town. That brought in the state police with bomb sniffer dogs and the Coast Guard which courageously, if a bit foolishly, put their own boats under the bridge as a first line of defense (or a better target). The call was eventually traced to a pay phone in Brunswick so a SWAT team was dispatched to remove the phone for fingerprint and DNA testing no doubt! After the scare, there were then eleven officers on scene at or near the school!

In addition, although I didn't see former president Jimmy Carter in attendance, I did see about 40 "international" (as least "from away") monitors and poll watchers who checked various voters for the proper credentials. Several young stern-men, probably sent by their lobstermen employers, were challenged, one for having a child in the Falmouth school system!

There was an almost circus atmosphere despite the security threats and all I could think about was a medieval fair. All sorts of people seldom seen out in daylight appeared. The night before, people assumed to be from Brunswick, put up hundreds and hundreds of bright yellow signs on many the telephone poles, illegal but highly visible, calling for Harpswell voters to "save the bay for their neighbors." Since Brunswick residents are widely regarded as coming yearly to rob Harpswell of its clams and lobsters, this tactic may not have been as successful as proponents had hoped! Another brave Brunswick lad walked the streets of Harpswell all day with a sign urging a "No" vote.

Signs and colorful slogans were everywhere. Most were, of course, about the LNG facility vote itself: "LNG Can't Buy Me," "Keep Your Pipe Out of My Bottom," "Fairwinds for Me" and "LNG Works for Me," as well as the prophetic "Fishing Families Count, Too." One sign stated simply, "Money Is the Root of All Upheaval," while another for a selectman candidate seemed to claim a huge portrait of Patrick Swayze had endorsed her. My favorite was a prominent "Free Martha" sign, no doubt from a resident who shops regularly at Kmart.

I also liked the bumper strip which read "Get a taste of religion, lick a witch." I wasn't exactly sure what that meant but two laughing women asked me when I came out of the polling booth, "Did you see any witches in there, sonny?" So I guess there was even a local coven in action that day.

Some people were upset about the number of police in the area, for as one told me, "We're not savages after all." But a poll watcher insisted they were needed, assuring me, "There has been a home invasion on Orrs Island," although she did not indicate which side had mounted such an offensive action in the middle of this fine voting morning.

What a crazy and amazing time.

For forty years, I have told my students of government that high voter turnout is a bad thing, a sure sign of systemic pathology, that the body politic is so really riled up that both sides view the election as a zero sum game. Those of you who doubt this proposition, think of Weimar Germany where the communists, the socialists and the Nazis all thought that if they lost the election they would lose their life style *and* their lives. So in the elections during the rise of Hitler, voter turnout was over 90% in all elections because so much was perceived to be at stake.

So too with Harpswell. It was widely believed by supporters that if Fairwinds passed, over $1.2 billion would come the town's way and that property taxes would be cut in half, if not eliminated totally. Conversely, many fisherman and lobstermen whose livelihood depends on the bay in question believed that the project would destroy the environment and drive them out of business.

Angry partisans actually got quite creative: in addition to relentlessly ripping down and defacing hundreds and hundreds of signs over a three month period, some wits even put their opponents' houses and boats for sale in Uncle Henry's weekly at ridiculously low prices! The resulting deluge of phone inquiries drove the targets mad.

With these perceived stakes, voter turnout was extremely high. A record 2000 (60%) number voted absentee and 70% of all eligible voters cast ballots. Some said the vote total would have been higher except for the bomb scare!

In the end, the Blessed Mother of Economic Growth lost out to the forces of King Neptune by a margin of 55% to 45%,

and a good time was had by one and all.

As for the "Free Martha" campaign, the results of that effort are not in just yet.

A CASCADE OF IRONIES

Sometimes political irony is so stupendous that it takes your breath away.

The current machinations of the Maine Legislative leadership in are in this category. While professing to want to defeat the 1% tax cap proposal of Carol Palesky, they are actually pushing for a June vote on the issue, a move that will virtually assure passage of the measure.

Why is June rather than November the absolute wrong time for those who wish to defeat the tax cap proposal?

At least six reasons leap to mind:

First, the Republican portion of a June vote will feature a much more conservative cohort than in the general election (perhaps as high as 40%). Conservatives simply vote in Republican primaries in greater percentages than they do in the general election. They are also the Republicans most likely to support the tax cap.

Second, the Democratic portion of that June vote contains a relatively high proportion of conservatives as well. It is one of the great myths of Maine politics that liberals dominate Democratic primaries. With astonishingly few exceptions, the more moderate or even conservative of Democratic candidates usually wins statewide and second CD contests. Think of John Baldacci, think of Mike Michaud. And remember Joe Brennan, even later in his career when he was defeated for statewide office, easily won his nominations against more liberal opponents, including Tom Allen.

Third, the reason for this moderate-conservative voting pattern is the importance of the Franco-American vote in Democratic primaries. Franco-American voters are the most conservative of all that party's building blocs and currently favor the tax cap by wide margins. The Franco American vote for tax cap will be decisive this June.

Fourth, Democrats who dislike the cap but expect to get a boost from a high Portland area turnout are in for a shock. That is because the voters of Portland—liberal, moderate and conservative—have just received the jolt of their property taxes going up 150% to 250% in a single year! Do not look for a liberal landslide in Portland to bail out an anti-tax cap coalition in June.

Fifth, the able leaders of the cap campaign, Phil Harriman and Eric Cianchette, will be able to draw on substantial Republican and business financial support for their campaign. They will raise more money and faster money than their opponents, a big advantage in a short campaign of less than six weeks. The tax cap proposal already has very wide and deep support; it will not take much to hold that support for a few weeks no matter what the anti-tax cap forces do.

Sixth, tax caps can be defeated but it takes considerable time to erode the support for the idea of a quick and simple tax fix that can't be tampered with by politicians. It also takes a lot of money, usually a 2–1 advantage, something that will simply not be possible for the anti-side if the election is held in June. A long campaign, not a short one, favors the opposition.

So, those who don't want a tax cap are doing what is most likely to result in one.

But what about those who favor a tax cap? They, too, have it completely backwards. Carol Palesky and her followers don't want the election in June when they have the best chance of winning. They want it in November when they have far less chance!

How's that for a double irony?

But back to the Legislative leadership. Why are they making this truly dumb move? Democrats simply don't want to run against both Republicans and the attractions of the tax cap from now until November while Republicans seem to both want the tax cap on the ballot now but not later. Democrats are even thinking of putting a competing measure on the ballot in June. This is another very bad idea.

While it is extremely unlikely that their proposal for a one cent increase in the sales tax would beat a tax cap—I have truly never heard of any tax beating an anti-tax proposal in the same election—it is possible that a confusing competing measure would hold down the Palesky proposal to a plurality. This would simply ensure that it is on the ballot again—in November when they're all running!

A final irony, a June vote will virtually assure the passage of the Palesky tax cap. And that will absolutely require a substantial raising of the sales and/or income tax, thus forcing Governor Baldacci to break his commitment to avoid adding to Maine's overall state and local tax burden.

The leadership in the Maine Senate seems hell-bent on making Baldacci the only Democratic governor (except Clinton Clausen who died in office) since World War II to have but a single term.

The lunacy of it all does rather take your breath away.

Postscript: The Governor listened to good advice and insisted that the referendum be decided in November in the general election and with no competing measure on the ballot. The so-called Palesky referendum was crushed 64% to 36%. See the following chapter entitled "The Big Winner."

QUEEN OF THE NORTH—AND SOUTH

Note: In this referendum, a Yes vote would have banned the use of baiting, trapping or dogs to kill a bear. A No vote would have allowed these three methods to continue in use.

With apologies to Arturo Peres-Reverte, whose *Queen of the South* is the best book I have read in several years, I am dubbing Edith "Edie" Smith Leary "Queen of the North" for this election cycle. She is already "Queen of the South" for her performance as campaign manager last year in the Casinos No! campaign. Edie, who heads up the Eaton Peabody Consulting Group and her field director, Will Gardiner, defied the odds and carried the day.

Gardiner, the 14,500 members of Maine's Fish and Wildlife Conservation Council, The Maine Professional Guides Association, the Maine Trappers Association, the Sportsman's Alliance of Maine, and Eve Rice and the 975 women of SWIM (Sporting Women in Maine) did a terrific, even unprecedented, job in developing a powerful grass roots ground game and donating very significant amounts to keep the No team electorally competitive.

Edie was the overall campaign manager for the No On Two campaign and what a campaign she ran! Facing an almost impossible challenge and a well-financed National Humane Society effort to eliminate bear baiting, hounding and trapping, she put together a truly extraordinary effort.

I have been involved nearly 100 campaigns over the last 25 years and I can state categorically that they are by their very nature, chaotic, tension-ridden, and centrifugal. Many can—and do—turn into "The Campaign from Hell." By contrast, this one was the most well run in my entire experience. "The Campaign from Heaven" is what insiders justly called it. It was a textbook operation and Edith Leary was the savvy force that kept it all together.

Edie and her brother, the executive director of SAM, George Smith, also put on a fund raising clinic, going from nowhere to over $1 million from people from all over Maine and the United States who saw the referendum as a direct threat to their hunting heritage. Every time the National Humane Society upped the ante, they matched it. Every time the National Humane Society floated in new TV buys under the radar, they caught them in the act.

George Smith tapped into his national contacts to make sure that they realized what was at stake in Maine. Rob Sexton and the U.S. Sportsmen's Alliance, Sandy and Joe Hosmer of the Safari Club International and many others such as Skip Trask and Ed and Cate Pineau responded to the call as well.

Governor Baldacci, too, deserves a great deal of credit. When the bear biologist and other members of the Maine Department of Inland Fisheries and Wildlife were threatened with a gag order and even some of his own staff wanted him to stay out of the fray, the Governor stood tall and supported his notion of "science, not emotion or politics" should determine game management in the state of Maine.

He insisted that the people who know the bears the best needed to be heard. Dick Davies and Paul Jacques were also invaluable in the entire effort, as was the Department of Inland Fisheries and Wildlife who stood up to those who would make game management a perpetual political food fight.

The media consultant, Erik Potholm rightly anticipated that the proponents would use the most graphic and heart wrenching scenes and he countered with a very effective series of ads featuring wildlife professionals. These powerful commercials turned a 2–1 deficit into a 54% to 46% victory. He remains undefeated in Maine ballot measures with nine victories in a row.

The media stars of the No side included the state's bear biologist, Jennifer Vashon, who taught the cruel yuppies of the south a valuable lesson, Jack Knight, Gloria Curtis, Craig McLaughlin and Tenley Meara, Bowdoin's own registered Maine Guide—all of whom projected credibility and authority.

For his part, Dave Emery did a truly magnificent job in his tracking polls, picking up even small movements along the voter net. He is one of the few pollsters who are consistently able to project outcomes when the voting patterns are turnout driven. Seldom has anyone so carefully calculated an election outcome with such a high voter turnout. In this case, the higher the turnout the better for the No forces and on election day, as Maine voters hit the 75% level, the tide turned decisively. Emery was once again right on target.

In terms of the print media, Maine's premier out door writers such as Paul Reynolds and Tom Hennessey were effective in combating the propaganda and emotional attacks of non-hunters. With the exception of the *Portland Press Herald*, all the major dailies urged a NO vote. The Portland papers weighted in heavily in support of the Yes side in editorials, columns and reporting but then had the gall to refuse to have their editorial board even meet with opponents, including the state's bear biologist! A sad day for balanced journalism indeed.

It was a tough, hard, bruising campaign with many dimensions, rather like playing chess on 5 or 6 boards at once. Through it all, Edie Smith Leary masterfully controlled the action, directed the allocation of resources and kept her side on the winning strategy. The NO side lost only Cumberland and York counties and tied in Sagadahoc. All the other counties voted NO with Aroostok leading the way with 65% of the vote.

Thanks to her efforts, "The Wild, Wild East" lives and Edith Leary is truly the Queen of the North and Queen of the South.

THE DYNAMICS OF POLITICAL LEADERSHIP

INTRODUCTION

What constitutes leadership? What makes for "good" versus "bad" leadership? Are there any particular "Maine" qualities which interact to produce the former or the latter?

Maine has always produced quite an amazing number of national political figures as well as a very strong in-state cohort. In fact, when you look at the history of Maine and the United States, you might be stunned to see what a considerable impact a small (population) state like Maine has had on the national scene. One of the chapters in this section highlights the long tradition of Mainers doing important work both in the state and at the national level.

What is fascinating about the political process, however, is to try to determine who will emerge as the next important leader in Maine's political firmament.

Often that is not easy to do while the process of individual maturation is going on. Nor are political heroes always fortunate enough to fit the issues of their particular time. While subsequent chapters point out those who not only provided important leadership and who are rightly given public acclaim for their activities, we should also note the political figures who were out of favor when they exhibited leadership, but subsequent events proved them correct.

In this regard, I always think of two contemporary Maine figures, former Senator Bill Hathaway and former Congressman Dave Emery. Both were defeated in senate races because they showed courage and conviction to take unpopular, but eventually correct issue positions.

Hathaway, for example, lost to Bill Cohen in 1978 in significant part because of his stands favoring both the Maine Indian Land Claims settlement and the returning of the Panama Canal to Panama. While these stands displeased voters at the time, both came to pass and are now regarded as having been the right thing to do by most Mainers today.

Likewise, Dave Emery lost his bid for the U.S. Senate in 1984 because of his very strong support for both the Reagan tax cuts and the enormous military buildup during Reagan's first administration. He could not have held these views at a more inopportune time, but he believed they were the right positions and played an important and visible role in a leadership position in Congress to support both politics. He lost his senate bid, but the policies prevailed and proved enormously critical to the subsequent military and economic success of the United States.

Another, more contemporary, example would be the leadership provided by Maine's present governor, John Baldacci. He currently gets little public credit for his courageous efforts to make Maine's government run more efficiently and to bring Maine's public policy into more realistic balance with its ongoing revenue stream.

Republicans object to his style and claim his policies do not go far enough in cutting government spending, but many progressive Democrats object that he is cutting programs too deeply (or in some cases at least not expanding them fast enough).

At the same time, he has not hesitated to take on his own political base by opposing an Indian gambling casino in the state or property tax proposals which he believes do more harm than good. At this writing, he stands at a hinge of history, however, with an opportunity to change Maine's government more substantially than any governor since Ken Curtis in the late 1960's.

Leadership is not always apparent at first encounter and some legacies are more enduring than others. The chapters which follow explore many dimensions of leadership in the Pine Tree State and it remains for the reader to decide which elements of leadership are the most desirable from their point of view.

A CONTINUING TRADITION

It's pretty heady stuff.

When you read about the Maine men and women who have stood at the centers of power in the Pine Tree State and in the United States since 1776 and even in the Revolutionary War itself, you see that our Susan Collins, Olympia Snowe, Mike Michaud and Tom Allen stand at the end of a long line of those who provided distinguished service to the state and the country. Ultimately, their place in the Maine firmament invites comparisons with those who went before.

There is General Knox, Washington's chief of artillery and major factor in his successful campaign to capture and hold Trenton, New Jersey during that long winter at Valley Forge. And William King was one of the principal leaders of the separatist movement against Massachusetts, culminating on July 26, 1819 when Maine voted to split off from Massachusetts. He became Maine's first governor.

One also shouldn't forget Ester Biggs who in 1854 declared, "What can women do in the great crusade? Woman can agitate the slavery question." Harriett Beecher Stowe did, her "Uncle Tom's Cabin" galvanizing much of a nation against the evils of slavery. This prompted Lincoln to supposedly say upon meeting her, "So you're the little lady who started this big war."

In Lincoln's first administration, Maine's Hannibal Hamlin, was vice president during the Civil War, serving the state and the nation both after and before in the U.S. Senate. There was also Senator William Pitt Fessenden, whose crucial vote saved the presidency of Andrew Johnson. His vote is thought by some to have cost Fessenden his life due to the ensuing stress caused by attacks on him by radical Republicans for that vote.

Maine, it should be remembered, sent a higher percentage of its men (and some women) to fight in the Civil War than any other northern state. Maine also provided a number of men who became important generals during that war, including the celebrated Joshua Chamberlain, Adelbert Ames, Israel Washburn and the often-overlooked Oliver Otis Howard. After the war, Howard became head of the newly created Freedman's Bureau in charge of the freed African Americans and in addition, he was the founder of Howard University.

And few Mainers loomed larger on the national scene following the American Civil War than James Blaine, editor of the *Kennebec Journal* and Republican political boss and eventual donor of the future home of Maine governors. Blaine came within a precious few electoral votes of winning the White House in 1884. He also contended for that office in 1876, 1880 and 1888, and had a distinguished additional career as U.S. Secretary of State.

Another impressive national figure from that era is Thomas Bracket Reed, known as "Czar" Reed when he was Speaker of the U.S. House. Reed was the creator of the rules of order of that body, which still prevail today. A person of great integrity, he resigned his position in opposition to the imperialistic effort of the Spanish American War. He was also an early and outspoken champion of women's rights and civil service reform.

1889 was something of a high tide of Maine influence in Washington with Maine men holding the positions of Chief Justice of the Supreme Court (Melville Fuller), president of the Senate (Eugene Hale), and chair of the powerful House Ways and Means Committee (Nelson Dingley).

Paul Mills also provides an important nominee for this tradition. He adds Lillian M.N. Stevens, who from 1898 to 1914 was the president of the Woman's Christian Temperance Union with 500,000 members nationwide. She also worked hard for women's rights, especially the vote.

Also, Democrat Charles F. Johnson was chosen senator in 1911, the first Democrat to serve in the U.S. Senate since 1857. He later served on the prestigious U.S. Circuit Court of Appeals in Boston. Sumner Sewall, who would become governor from 1941 to 1945, served with distinction in the First World War, becoming an air ace in combat by shooting down seven German planes.

And no list of Maine leaders and visionaries could omit Governor Percival Baxter, who was governor from 1921 to 1925 and whose legacy includes the environmental essential of Maine, Baxter State Park, a truly enduring legacy.

We certainly can't forget Lewiston's own Louis J. Brann who won two terms as governor in 1932 and 1934 at the height of the depression. Brawn was the only Democratic governor to be elected from 1914 until Edmund S. Muskie in 1954.

After World War II the cast includes Edmund S. Muskie, of course, and Margaret Chase Smith, who both usher in the modern period of Maine politics as the leaders against whom subsequent national figures such as Bill Cohen, George Mitchell, Olympia Snowe and Susan Collins, all major national figures in their own right, continue to be measured.

Margaret Chase Smith was the first woman ever put into nomination for president of the United States (1964) and a tireless worker on behalf of the state no matter what the personal cost. As the controversy continues about Rep. Tom Allen's ill-conceived and hurtful resignation from the House Armed Services Committee, it would be wise to remember that Margaret Chase Smith once served with distinction as well as simultaneously on the Senate Armed Services *and* Appropriations committees. She, too, found the work burdensome, even onerous, but very necessary for the interests of the state of Maine.

What do so many of the above all share? They were possessors of great courage, conviction and conscience and foresight. All served the state and all tried to do whatever they could, at whatever the personal cost and sacrifice to advance the cause of Maine at the national level.

It's a very impressive heritage.

Those running for political office in the Pine Tree State have a political pedigree of the first order as well as some grand role models. Let's hope that those running for office in 2004 live up to that legacy.

VINDICATION

As the 2002 election for governor moves forward, all five candidates who want to replace Angus King would do well to examine the reasons for his amazing popularity. His 70% approval rating remains the highest of any governor in post World War II Maine and among current governors all over the United States. Unlike congresspeople and senators, whose popularity is much easier to maintain, most sitting governors would kill for an approval rating over 55%.

Yet King has not been afraid to take bold and controversial steps and stands. He has not shied away from doing what was right rather than what was expedient. Now, as he enters his last six months in office, we can begin to see the outlines of his legacy.

His laptop program is proving to be both outstanding and of vital importance for the future of our children. Angus King is too much of a gentleman to blow his own horn. But his laptop idea has hit a home run. The early results from the prototype schools that tried it this spring have been phenomenal. The response to the laptops has been fantastic, overwhelmingly positive.

As a lifelong educator, I applauded his laptop idea from the first time I heard about it. I think, though, it was a mistake to have the story break in the *Boston Globe* and *Wall Street Journal* rather than the Maine press. The Maine press corps has not treated the idea kindly and has given wide coinage to legislator who opposed the idea, no matter how bizarre their basis for opposition.

The misguided and often mean-spirited opposition to the program has continued until this moment. From "Give them all a chainsaw instead" to "Let them eat laptops," people who should have known better have taken pot shots at the concept and its implementation as well as its $37 million price tag. In that regard, I think it would be worth it at twice the price.

Even now, two extremely short sighted legislators, Republicans Philip Cresey Jr. and Brian Duprey, are trying to see if the state of Maine can break its contract with Apple Computer and wreak the program. How wrong headed and how unfair to the children of Maine! As a Republican who believes in giving everyone a chance to make the most out of themselves, I'm embarrassed at their penny wise and pound-foolish attitudes toward a genuine boon.

Teaching at Bowdoin College for thirty years, I can honestly say my greatest satisfaction and psychic rewards come from taking students from impoverished backgrounds with no parent having gone to college, and seeing them grasp their own upside potential, their own packet of positive possibilities and have them use education as a pathway of upward mobility. To see students expand their intellectual, emotional and career horizons is extremely rewarding, and for society, extremely positive.

Having a laptop in the hands of every seventh and eighth grade student in Maine will open up the world for each and every one. It gives them the whole world—past, present and future—as well as the opportunity to grow and learn and up their aspirations and dreams. It is a revolution that will impact the lives of every student.

For ultimately, that is what the laptop does, it widens the inner and world horizon of every student. It takes computers from being just a classroom tool to a life-changing stimulus to a better life, a better world, and a better future.

But this spring's results go beyond that wonderful set of goals. The laptops simply improve classroom performance all across the board. The pilot programs from this year—which put 868 iBooks in Portland, Kittery, Auburn, Boothbay, Readfield, Bar Harbor, Guildford, Pembroke and Presque Isle—have been amazingly successful.

Look at some of these results: in Boothbay, special education teacher

Kim O'Brien said the laptops "leveled the playing field" for many students with disabilities." All students using laptops showed improvement in many areas where it hadn't been anticipated.

For example, in Boothbay, absence days dropped from 247 to 67, tardiness dropped from 199 to 56. In Pembroke, detentions dropped from 28 to 3, suspensions went from 5 to 0 and grades improved tremendously. 91% of students improved in one academic area, 82% improved in two academic areas and 73% improved in three or more subject areas. These are stunning results.

Also, students perceived that learning was more interesting and that their teachers had become more interesting as well! In Boothbay, for example, 90% of student claimed that school was more interesting after the laptops arrived and 88% said the teachers "taught better" while 92% said the subject were much more interesting.

These are truly remarkable outcomes.

Teachers and parents all across the state should move to impeach or recall any legislator who would gut this program.

The laptop project is nothing less than a true educational revolution for all the kids of Maine. Regardless of the income of their parents or the remoteness of their schools, Maine students will now have a chance to grasp the future and make it their own, to gain aspirations and performance opportunities.

It is a revolution of both expectations and performance.

Angus, the improved educational opportunities and enhanced futures of the children of Maine will be your finest legacy.

Don't let shortsighted legislators gut the program that makes the future so exceptional for all Maine students.

STATESMAN?

In Twelfth Night, Shakespeare has Malvolio utter one of the great epithets of all time, one we can apply with profit to political figures. "Be not afraid of greatness. Some are born great. Some achieve greatness and some have greatness thrust upon them."

Which is Rick Bennet?

Six months ago, Bennett of Norway had a wide-open future. Many considered him the odds-on favorite to lead the Republican Party against John Baldacci in order to keep the Blaine House out of Democratic hands. Others considered him a winner for Baldacci's second Congressional seat.

Certainly, he would have been well positioned to capture that office, having already run once in the district, losing to Baldacci in 1994 by a narrow margin of 45.7% to 40.7% while John Michael, the Independent, got 8.8% and Charles Fitzgerald, the Green, 4.7%.

Speculation about his future was further stimulated by his agreement with Senator Mike Michaud to be Senate President during the 2002 legislative session and by his highly publicized political maneuvering during the budget debate when he seemed to make war on both Governor King and the Democratic controlled House.

But in the end, Bennett ran for neither office. First he dropped out of the governor's race, declaring somewhat disingenuously that he was not ready for an executive position. Cynics thought it likely that he had not seen any encouraging polls in a match-up against Baldacci, but others thought he had decided to run for Congress.

But there are only two basic types of Maine political figures. There are the "Washingtonians," politicians who much prefer living in the nation's capitol and playing—however tangentially—a national role to living in the state and being governor. Bill Cohen, Dave Emery, George Mitchell, Tom Andrews, Tom Allen, and Olympia Snowe are all Washingtonians.

Then there are the "Blaine House aspirants", those who dislike living in Washington and want to be governor or nothing. Notable examples of the "Blaine House aspirants" include Joe Brennan and John Baldacci (even though both served in Congress, neither liked it), Angus King, Jim Longley, and Ken Curtis.

Only Jock McKernan belongs in both categories, liking Washington and the Blaine House equally.

Citing family concerns, Bennett astonished many political reporters and observers by dropping out of the second CD Congressional race on July 11. Only those who were at the Moxie celebration on July 7 in Lisbon were not surprised. 25,000 people were there, as well as most of his opponents and no appearance by Bennett? The handwriting was on the wall and insiders buzzed with anticipation all that weekend.

Bennett had been the front-runner for the Republican nomination for Maine's second Congressional District. Now there will be a wide-open race. Popular Bangor Mayor Tim Woodcock brings the most governmental experience and gravitas to the race. Kevin Raye of Jonesport is young, energetic and possesses a keen appreciation for the political game and initial big bucks. Stavros Mendros of Lewiston will be a dynamic and always interesting counter-point to either of the other two, both in terms of issues such as right to life, and in terms of style. With Mendros in the race, Dick Campbell of Holden may run but perhaps shouldn't.

But back to Bennett. He has freed himself up to be more important on the Maine political scene. He has actually strengthened his hand for influencing Maine's public policy in the years ahead.

It was never clear to me how he would run for Congress effectively and be Senate President at the same time. I thought Mike Michaud had made a smart bargain by being President of the Senate in 2001 and not in 2002.

Having his potential rival tied to Augusta while he roamed the district would have been a big plus for Michaud.

Now Bennett is free to put his considerable talents to work fashioning public policy and playing a major role in making the State Senate Republican. Many Democratic insiders would have much preferred to have him out on the campaign trail for Congress than actively leading a major effort to elect Republican state senators.

Almost single handedly, Bennett kept the Republicans close in the State Senate last election cycle. Now that his position depends on it, he will pursue the goal of a Republican Senate with even more zeal. Democrats are neither pleased nor amused. And the King administration cannot be happy at the prospect of dealing with a focused and energized Bennett.

Herein lies to rub for Rick Bennett, however. Bright and articulate, he must be partisan and ruthless enough to lead the Republicans to victory in 2002. But can he also be a statesman, putting good public policy ahead of personal or partisan agenda?

Does Rick Bennett have the vision to use his newly liberated power for the good of all Maine people?

I hope so. With two dozen—or more—people busy running for Congress and Governor, and in the twilight of the King administration, Rick Bennett could do a lot of good for the state. Or he could play a lot of ego games and fail to live up to his potential. Bennett dropped out of the various races to devote more time and energy to his family and for that, we can only give him high marks. His legacy as President of the Maine Senate, however, will be enduring only if he cares enough for the rest of the families of Maine and focuses his considerable talents on improving their lives.

Malvolio would like his positioning but would wait to see the results.

ODE TO JOHN

He was a man of many parts.

A Yale graduate who made a living for some years digging clams and gillnetting fish. A decorated war hero who spent 35 missions in combat in extremely dangerous situations who was profoundly a man of peace. A long time avid hunter who hung up his guns and led a referendum to stop the hunting of moose, but never became anti-hunting. A speaker with a gruff, often harsh sounding voice who could write like an angel. A voice to challenge and provoke, but also a messenger who could soothe and calm.

John Cole was all of these and more.

A transplant to Maine from Long Island, he became one of Maine's foremost boosters and his love of the state was legendary. I remember once listening to him wax eloquent about the people of Maine on PBS to the point where a frustrated tourist from New York called in and accused him of promoting "hyper-nationalism of the type they have in Bosnia." All that did, of course, was to give John an opportunity for another long riff about the virtues of Maine people. He loved the state and its people with a fierce and enduring pride and he had an especially profound appreciation of the durability and strength of those who live in its rural settings.

He will forever be associated with the *Maine Times*, a counter culture (or more accurately perhaps, a counter establishment) paper he founded with Peter Cox. For many years, it was the paper the political class of Maine had to read. Delivered to the Legislature and executive branch in Augusta every Thursday, *The Maine Times* dominated the conversations of the capitol for the whole weekend and beyond. Read if it infuriated you, read if you loved it, but read it you must. You simply could not ignore it. You simply had to know what was in that—for many—"damned" *Maine Times*. John Cole was an inspired editorial leader as well as a writer of national prominence and he got his staff to do truly important and perspicacious pieces.

John was, at least in the environmental sense, a vital leader and gadfly both. He was also an interesting blend of liberal and conservative. Certainly, his primary hero was Ed Muskie, not only for his environmental stance but also for his crusty personification of the "best of Maine." But John also saw promise in other leaders—such as Bob Monks, Joe Sewall, and Bill Cohen—from all portions of the Maine political spectrum. If he thought you were a demagogue, and he did think that of Governor Jim Longley, he could be brutal and relentless. And he never had much good to say about George W. Bush or Margaret Chase Smith.

I feel very fortunate to have known John for thirty years. I have delighted in his political observations and his sense of Maine history and culture, his knowledge of the natural world and his almost religious veneration of it. I have read all of his books, often more than once, including his incredibly incisive and profoundly valuable work, "Fish of My Years," which really sums up the man and the legend. I hope his publisher will reissue it in paperback now as a tribute to all of his writing.

This past year, while working on my forthcoming book, "This Splendid Game," about the important electoral turning points of Maine politics, I had a chance to extensively interact with him about the last forty years of Maine history and have the wonderful experience of getting his insights chapter by chapter. I loved arguing with him and learning from him and seeing his childlike wonder when he too learned something new or previously hidden.

For that, ultimately, was John Cole's charm. He was always learning and always welcoming new knowledge. He knew a great deal, but always wanted to learn more. With his passing, I shall miss many things, but none more than this sense of wonder. His weekly column on nature was always interesting, always captivating, always filled with the insights which help us appreciate that Maine environment we all talk about and the natural world which so fascinates those of us who love Maine the way he did.

Interacting with his observers who called in bits of arcane information and wildlife sightings ("Why did the cute little red squirrel eat the baby bird?" "Because the nuts weren't ready."), and laced with the wonderfully loving relationship he had with his wife Jean (affectionately called "The Boss" in the column), John wove together a rich and profound tapestry of the natural world and drew us into it no matter what our previous state of mind.

More than any other writer in my experience, John Cole could tune into the natural world with the knowledge of a lifetime generated by a very smart and observant person coupled with the delicious wonder of a child.

It is that childlike wonder at the rhythms of nature and the process by which we are all integrated into the mysterious pulses of the universe that is his finest legacy.

John, you are already deeply, even inexplicably missed but we gain solace from the knowledge that you are still part of those marvelous rhythms and processes you spent a lifetime bringing to us and that your words of natural guidance will remain as long as there are libraries.

Your legacy is beloved and enduring.

BED AND POLITICAL BREAKFAST

I suppose I should say at the outset that I have a strong prejudice against bed and breakfast establishments. I mean, aren't most of them run by people who really don't like other people in their homes and are only doing it because of the big tax advantages?

I've honestly never had a really great time in a bed and breakfast and my recent experience was no exception. First, it looked like a jail and the people who owned it acted as if, at $100 a night, it was the bargain of the century. After we arrived at 4pm, they soon disappeared, never to reappear until breakfast.

Moreover, we were the only other guests in the dark and gloomy place. This should have been the tip off. No wonder, it was—at best—50 degrees in our room and never got any warmer all night long even though I went downstairs and turned up the central heat full blast. I ended up sleeping in my clothes. The next morning my wife foolishly tried to take a shower. The water was so cold she got a massive headache. It never got warm!

So we were in foul humor when we went down for "breakfast." I use that term most loosely. My dry cereal was very stale and the man portion of the team seemed to really resent it when I asked for a second glass of orange juice. Didn't get it of course; for when the grinning fellow returned, it was with a grudging one third of a refill. I did drink massive amounts of hot water tea, something I usually only do when I'm ill.

But nothing, and I mean nothing, prepared us for the onslaught of the female portion of the jailer team. She began to rant and rave about George W. Bush and could not be stopped. Now my wife is actually pretty nonpolitical, but she does like Laura Bush and thinks she is a credit to the U.S. of A. Even in Democratic dominated Brunswick, she usually gets a nod of approval for fondness for Laura.

But not from this hostess. I mean she tore into Laura for supporting "that cretin," a phrase I eventually figured out was directed at our president. She began with a screed about how "he stole the election" and went right onto how "he wrecked the economy" and that "he's completely mismanaged the war against terror" and ended up—and I'm not making this up—with the phrase, "we have to shoot him in the knees" when I pointed out that in the last election, a lot of people seemed to like his message.

When I asked whether post September 11 would have been better handled had Gore been elected, she insisted he had been, but then dismissed Gore as "a buffoon." Turns out she felt only Hillary Clinton as president could get the job done right in fighting terrorism! Now I have to admit this is the first live human being I've heard espouse this bizarre notion. But boy, wouldn't it be fun to see W versus Hillary in 2004. No dullness there!

Regrettably, we had to race off and catch a ferry so I was unable to deliver the fulmination that was building as I listened to this utter nonsense. But I later reflected on the incredibly strange notion that the United States needs new and "better" leadership on the terrorist front.

What I want to ask is this, isn't the war against terror going very well? Have I missed something? Haven't the bad guys been driven out of Afghanistan with amazingly light American casualties? Aren't predator drones looking for and killing terrorists here and there and haven't thousands of suspects been swept off the streets in dozens of countries? Aren't we busting up cells all over the world and shutting off their lines of credit?

Now I know they *could* strike tomorrow at some soft target in the United States but in the sixteen months since September 11, 2001, haven't they been operationally unable to strike the territory of the United States? I am truly sorry they are still blowing up synagogues in Tunisia, hotels in Kenya, French tankers at sea and nightclubs in Bali but from our national point of view, isn't that infinitely better than having them blow up something in St. Louis or Chicago or Los Angeles?

It is true that most of us would like to see Osama Bin Laden hanging upside down from the Statue of Liberty by now but this is a ten to twenty year struggle. It's just begun. I think we all should put partisanship aside and keep it there and have a little patience.

Postscript: When on our way to Islesboro recently, my wife and I went by the place we affectionately refer to as "the prison," we found it closed and the building for sale. Many, people, one assumes, do not like political commentary with stale Corn Flakes.

"ANYBODY BUT BUSH"?

It's truly unbelievable.

I probably know too many liberal Democrats. But still, "Bush Bashing" this year seems to have gone over the top.

Never, ever—not even in the heyday of Nixon hatred—in my experience have Democrats in Maine and nationally gone so nuts over a Republican figure. He is the Prince of Darkness. He is Darth Vader. He is The Devil's Spawn. The hatred of rabid Democrats is palpable.

The Patriot Act? A heinous crime against America. Keeping terrorists at Guantanamo Bay? A heinous crime against humanity. The Department of Homeland Security? A bad joke. Any credit for throwing bin Laden out of Afghanistan and getting rid of the Taliban? Forget it, America's amazing success in Afghanistan is considered almost irrelevant or simply all lost in the Iraqi sauce. Dethroning and catching Saddam, the man who killed more Moslems than anyone else in history? Who cares? Libya gives up weapons of mass destruction? Only because Bush isn't being Bush!!!! The President simply gets no credit for any of his many accomplishments in the global war on terror.

Recently, I have even seen a number of bumper strips which say "Anybody But Bush." That captures the irrational way many, if not most, D's are judging Bush.

"Anybody but Bush"? When it comes to leading the fight against global terror, I find it nearly impossible to imagine a majority of American voters believing that any of the Democratic candidates could do a better job or have a more efficacious strategic vision.

Al Sharpton? Please.

Dennis Kucinich? Pretty please.

Howard Dean? Anyone who complains about the American presidential primary system should look at this case history exposing a candidate variously termed, "A prairie dog on speed" and "Mr. Rogers with rabies." This man should not be entrusted with the office of first selectman in a small Maine town, let alone have his finger on the nuclear trigger.

Wes Clark? He now says we didn't need to go to war against Saddam Hussein. He says—with a straight face—"I would simply have gone and arrested him"! We often forgive naiveté among our generals but this piece of foolishness goes beyond the pale. And please remember, Clark is the only person I know of ever fired by Bill Cohen, one of nature's all times softies. How's that for a negative recommendation?

Joe Lieberman? I simply don't understand why he is running. And I suspect no one else does either, and soon, he won't be.

John Kerry? An often epigonic chap seemingly controlled by his vibrant and powerful wife and his media handler. He was very, very lucky in Iowa. Joe Trippi got it right on election night in Iowa: "Gephart killed his own campaign and he almost killed Dean's." Besides, it will be child's play to paint anyone who votes with Ted Kennedy nearly 100% of the time as another Massachusetts ultra-liberal. In his beginning is his end.

John Edwards? Could be the best of a poor lot I think. He may not be quite ready for prime time, but he seems to have the grace under pressure we require in these troubled times. Also, strategically he would be Bush's toughest opponent since he would challenge the President in his base areas. But in their present state of near-mania, liberal Democrats seem quite unlikely to nominate someone with that much whiff of Dixie this time around.

So.

Anybody but Bush?

I don't think so

Bush's State of the Union message said it all:

> We are at war. We need the will to persevere. We need an ongoing emphasis on power, security, and force projection. We need to finish the job, fight the international terrorists wherever they are and protect our homeland by taking the fight to the enemy. We need a leader who will stand fast and firm and get the job done and not be dismayed by setbacks or unpopularity. We need someone who recognizes the centrality of security to our future.

I know there are some Democrats who would rather see another 9/11 than give Bush credit for setting in motion policies to prevent another terrorist attack. Certainly they seem almost joyful about any setback in Iraq. They want Bush to fail so badly they wish calamity without end in order to prove their point. Or they want to abandon Iraq as soon as possible.

In this regard, it is enormously naïve to assume that militant terrorists from whatever society would call off their war simply because the United States withdrew from Iraq and/or stopped projecting its power globally. In fact, I would argue that it is the global reach of the United States that is what is standing between the world and much greater and more destructive levels of violence. How much better it is to fight al Qaeda in Baghdad than in Chicago.

We are in a decades-long contest of wills with a group of dangerous, ruthless global adversaries. If we do not prevail over the course of this struggle, we shall be subject to continuing and escalating attacks. It is impossible to protect the United States proper from every possible terrorist plot and plan. It is therefore necessary to continue the forward strategy that seeks out terrorists wherever they are and neutralizes them before they strike in this country. We must succeed in this or face a most unpleasant future.

The powerful rhetoric of Bush's State of the Union message resonates loud and clear over the din of petty and partisan minds: The first priority of the Republic is to defend itself. That is currently why the American people, by a 2–1 margin, say the Republicans are more trusted to handle security matters, without which nothing else matters.

Therefore . . .
National security is central to the future of this country.
And it is essential for our prosperity and progress.
In November, security will trump carping—and other issues.
That is why Bush will be re-elected.

NADER AND NEGATIVITY

It simply does not get any better than this.

Think about it.

A thoroughly discredited, saturnine, multi-millionaire with scruffy brown shoes and an ego the size of Australia decides to run for president. Despite having set back the national progress of one party for at least a decade, having elected a president he professes to abhor and having no known supporters among real voters, he is still determined to run for the nation's highest office again, this time as an "Independent." Bound and determined to produce a remake of "Groundhog Day," he sets off to re-elect the very target of his spiteful hatred and wild hyperbole!

It's truly both amazing and amusing.

Only in America!

Central casting in Hollywood could not come up with an odder duck in an odder scenario—or a more effective music score than the sound of him chanting, ominously and slowly, fervently and fast, high and low, irrespective of venue or audience: "Duopoly, duopoly, duopoly."

My God, Ralph Nader is running for president again.

When I wrote four years ago in this column (entitled "Run Ralphie Run"), I received much hate mail and calls from liberal Democrats who said my calling him both a "useful idiot" from the Republican point of view and an insurance policy for George W. Bush, was unkind, harsh, cruel and just plain wrong.

But when Ralphie delivered Florida, New Hampshire and the national election for Bush on cue, my early criticisms seemed mild in comparison to many of the epithets used by prominent wailers in the Democratic Party.

Now he's back at it again, pathetic and unwanted but nevertheless determined to repeat his historical blunder of monumental proportions (if you're a Democrat anyway). Is there anybody left in America who doesn't wonder how Nader got so rich supposedly fighting for the poor?

I wish Nader would drop out of the race so Bush could face and beat Kerry straight up with no assist from Nader. This time Bush won't need it.

Note to those who wrote, e-mailed and called about my last column concerning Bush, please be advised that I serve not the Republican Party, but the Norse god of mischief, Loki. Many of you also proved my very point by listing all the hyperbolic reasons, real and imaginary, why you are voting against our wonderful president.

Note also to all those who wrote, e-mailed and called to thank me for upholding the Republican conservative banner, you might want to withhold some of your applause until you read my future column on gay marriage!

But back to the business at hand.

Bush versus Kerry, the race is already shaping up as one for the history books.

It is going to be very, very negative from the very beginning. Remember, it's only February. When you see polling numbers like the ones which pertain today—with both guys at 45% and only 10% undecided—and when you see the "stacks" (the piling up of 12 or 15 reasons to vote against him) against Bush, you know that 10% is going to learn everything, and I mean everything, negative about the Kerry until the stacks are even.

The intense polarization of the electorate, based as it is on issues, ideology and even cosmology, requires that both candidates unload upon the other, constantly and with something beyond the usual mild hyperbole.

There is simply no other way to change the electoral balance and put either candidate over the top.

We can't do much but sit back and enjoy the process; it's going to set a modern indoor record for negative commercials from both parties. It's going to be a titanic, Manichean struggle rather like the one depicted in Stephen King's *The Stand.*

But fear not, however negative this year's presidential race becomes, no matter how much mud is slung and re-slung, it will have to go "a far piece" in order to match the cogency of President Ulysses S Grant's campaign slogan for Republicans of the post Civil War era: "Vote the Way You Shot."

The power of this slogan and its appeal to the memories of the American Civil War were echoed in the super-heated rhetoric of the 1870's as witnessed by the excerpts from a speech by Republican Robert G. Ingersoll (thanks to Joel Moser who sent to the quote to me from the Muskie Archives at Bates):

> Every man who endeavored to tear the old flag from the heaven that enriches it was a Democrat. Every man that tried to destroy this nation was a Democrat. Every enemy this great Republican has had for twenty years has been a Democrat. Every man who shot Union soldiers was a Democrat.
>
> Every man that raised bloodhounds to pursue human beings was a Democrat. Every man who helped to burn orphan asylums in New York was a Democrat. Every man who spread smallpox and yellow fever in the North was a Democrat." Soldiers, every scar, every arm that is lacking, every limb that is gone, every scar is a souvenir of a Democrat.
>
> Every soldier who drank out of a skull was a Democrat.

Now that's negative campaigning!

Nothing George W. Bush or Karl Rove or Lynn Cheney, let alone Terry McAuliffe or Teresa Heinz Kerry can come up with will even be in that ballpark. Nothing said this election cycle by either presidential ticket would come close to that level of vitriol.

I hope.

IN THE SHADOW OF MARGARET: THE PERSISTENCE OF AN ENDURING MAINE ARCHETYPE

June 1, 2004 will mark the 44th anniversary of Margaret Chase Smith's maiden—and most important—speech to the United States Senate. She was the first woman ever directly elected to that body in her own right without having filled a previous term of a senator husband.

Much has been written about Margaret Chase Smith's powerful and courageous "Declaration of Conscience" speech during which she stood up to the witch-hunt tactics of Senator Joseph McCarthy as well as the inherent intolerance of the communist ideology. Her words written almost five decades ago have power and impact even today:

> As a United States Senator, I am not proud of the way in which the Senate has been made a publicity platform for irresponsible sensationalism. I am not proud of the reckless abandon in which unproved charges have been hurled from this side of the aisle.

> The nation sorely needs a Republican victory. But I don't want to see the Republican Party ride to political victory on the Four Horsemen of Calumny—Fear, Ignorance, Bigotry and Smear.
>
> As an American, I condemn a Republican "fascist" just as much as I condemn a Democrat "communist." I condemn a Democrat "fascist" just as much as I condemn a Republican 'communist. They are equally dangerous to you and me and to our country.

But not all accounts underscore the incredible hold Senator McCarthy had over the political system at the time. Not only were Senate Republicans and Democrats paralyzed with fear, General Eisenhower and other prominent Republicans were afraid of McCarthy and did nothing to stop his febrile anti-communist smears until long after Margaret stepped forward. And President Harry S. Truman, usually so feisty and combative, hung back in a diffident, almost shy fashion.

Nearly alone, Margaret stood up to McCarthy in 1950 and the communist ideology she also abhorred. An interesting footnote to history: while six other moderate Republican senators originally signed on to her resolution before she gave her speech, within weeks, only one other—Senator Wayne Morse of Oregon—had not withdrawn his name after a McCarthy inspired backlash began. All the others fled the political battlefield with their tails between their legs.

Contemporary reaction to her speech varied widely. She received nationwide attention, and a great deal of praise. Bernard Baruch, for example, said that if a man had made that speech, he would be the next president of the United States. But many conservatives attacked her personally; and in Maine, while most editorial comment was positive, Guy Gannett and his newspaper said it had done more harm than good.

Moreover, the Republican leadership in the Senate punished her with poor committee assignments and McCarthy even induced a senate staffer and former aide to Maine's previous Republican senator, Owen Brewster, to run against her in the Republican primary of 1954. She won handily with 83% of the vote.

Margaret Chase Smith stood her ground and established herself firmly in the firmament of not only Maine but U.S. politics as well. Her reputation for moderation, courage and independence grew over the years. Often on the outs with the Eisenhower White House, she voted her conscience and for all Americans over and over. In 1960, she became the first woman to have her name officially put into nomination for president.

All this for a woman born in 1897 who barely graduated from high school, rose from poverty through hard work and a strong will to serve her state for 32 years.

Her independent stances and personal following as opposed to reliance on party regulars changed the nature of Republican politics in the Pine Tree State. Stan Tupper, Bill Cohen, Dave Emery and Jock McKernan all followed her model in relying on their own organizations rather than the Republican State Committee. Mert Henry, old enough to have been the leader of Youth for Margaret Chase Smith (1948) and young enough to have headed up the Senatorial campaign of Susan Collins (1996), put it succinctly: "If only the Republican State Committee had voted, Margaret would never have been elected to anything."

Although at age 75, she was eventually to lose to Congressman Bill Hathaway in 1972, her legacy endures today as both U.S. Senators, Olympia Snowe and Susan Collins have modeled their careers after her. They stand, as she did, for integrity, feistiness and independence, neither of them afraid to tangle with the presidents of their own party when they believe principle or Maine priorities are at stake.

Margaret's political shadow remains long, positive, inspiring and worthy of emulation. Although she was something of an anti-feminist feminist (and in my judgment, all the more interesting and effective for that ironic juxtaposition), all women and men in Maine politics owe her homage for being the trailblazer she was.

She began modern Maine politics in 1940. She set many political records during her lifetime. She was a strong feminist before the word was in vogue. Maine's two women senators today patterned themselves after her. Her legacy endures to the present day. Margaret Chase Smith remains the principle Maine political archetype for leadership. She is the standard against which all subsequent Maine Titans, Edmund S. Muskie, William S. Cohen and George Mitchell, measured themselves.

Margaret Chase Smith's story is surprisingly powerful, because in the very last analysis, she made herself into not only the prototype of the modern political figure in the Pine Tree State, her legacy of leadership continues to cast a long and healthy shadow over the politics of the state. More than any other figure in modern Maine politics Margaret Chase Smith set the independent standard against which all major political figures are still measured in the Pine Tree State.

END GAME

It is now that most delicious of times in politics: the End Game.

Here's where I think we are and what the trailing side in a variety of situations must do to win in Sun Journal land. As the 2004 general election winds down, here are my biased and personal readings on the races. I hope they will stimulate all readers to get out and vote.

Presidential Race: A statistical dead heat. The Francos are not sold on either candidate so the race is still up for grabs. Bush must break 30% + of this group to win, and in order to do that, he must emerge as the candidate to keep America safe if this conservative Democratic cohort is to provide him with his margin of victory in Maine.

For Kerry, he seemed to lose, and is now regaining, his gender advantage with women. Kerry *has* lost Maine men for good. But the President's lackluster, even weak, first debate performance, coupled with Kerry's Alpha Male Mandrill display, is sending women, especially those in the home, back to Kerry. Current advantage: Kerry, but with Bush still in the hunt.

PS: Note to the President, if you have Osama's head in a freezer on some aircraft carrier, now is the time to bring it out.

PPS: All would-be pundits need to know that the Second CD is now more Democratic than before due to the inclusion of Waterville and Winslow, and the First CD is now more Republican due to the influx of cruel Yuppie Republicans into York county. Why do you think Peter Cianchette carried the first CD and only the 2nd went for John Baldacci in 2002?

Second CD race: Michaud sits on the national bullseye because of the presidential race. Otherwise, Hamel would be getting very little in the way of national resources. Many Republican strategists believe that if Bush gets any points out of Maine, it could be in the second CD, so there will be a lot of motion on behalf of the GOP there. I think it is more likely that Bush will get either 4 or 0 of Maine's electoral votes.

Michaud has worked incredibly hard, and Hamel has yet to break through the general voter consciousness. Plus he is being guided by a national Republican strategy which seems to ill fit the second CD.

Hamel needs to have a stupendous debate cycle in order to get in the hunt. He will have money for TV, but Michaud has the ground game, the personality, the campaign team, the work ethic and Pat Eltman. Current Advantage: Michaud.

First CD race: National Republicans made a very poor choice to target Michaud rather than Allen. Michaud is a good fit for the second CD, Allen was out of sync with his own district when he walked off the Armed Service Committee, something no other Mainer in modern times has voluntarily done in a time of war. Far too liberal for the cruel yuppies of York Country, but getting a pass from the national Republicans and gets many votes from the style Yuppies along the coast. Last cycle, this CD voted for a pro-choice, fiscal conservative Republican in giving Peter Cianchette the nod over John Baldacci. This year they have a chance to choose another one.

Charlie Summers had the right mentality and dedication to be the best representative qua representative from the first CD since Dave Emery, the last holder of that position to truly represent the majority of his constituents. Look for him to close the gap in the coming weeks. Could be a missed opportunity: Republicans. Current advantage: Allen.

Tax Cap: This very bad idea had 58% of the vote in June. It would have passed easily in June when the memory of the do-nothing, solve-nothing, care-nothing-about-ordinary-folks Legislature failed ignominiously for a second session in a row. Now, however, the "send a message" appeal is beginning to fade. It's one thing to send a cost-free message to Augusta. It's another to cut fire and police and pay a lot more in income taxes for the privilege of sending that message.

Palesky forces have slightly less than 40% and are unlikely to build on this percentage unless a huge cohort of less likely voters, including the Independents who seldom vote, turn up to send a message, cost or no. A massive Yes TV buy during the last two weeks of the campaign however, could threaten the current assessment. Current advantage: *No side.*

Ban Bear Bating: The National Humane Society in Colorado saw a cheap, easy target in Maine in 2004. They had already pushed this ballot measure in a number of other states. Despite advice from some of their more astute supporters, they took a huge gamble and up fronted money to pay for the effort to challenge the basic psychographics of the "Wild, Wild East." Big mistake. The state's bear biologist is the best authority figure and she says, "Don't change the law, things are just right."

Bill Nemitz, the *Portland Press Herald* columnist who cannot seem to relate to anyone north of Yarmouth, has it all wrong—Ms. Vashon, Maine's bear biologist, may be pregnant (shame on you Bill for bringing her gender and her fecundity up as an issue!), but she is right. After all, she knows more about the Maine bear population than all of us put together. Does Nemitz really like the Yes side's grotesque "Sopranos Bear" ad? Or believe it? Let the bears eat honey and donuts but don't let them show up in school yards at recess time. Current advantage: No side.

Regardless of I, or anyone else, thinks, get out and vote. There are no excuses for staying home this cycle. November 2004 has something for every Mainer. November 2004 has something for every American.

THE BIG WINNER

It was the biggest challenge to his governorship and his second term prospects.

The Democratic controlled Legislature, with a great deal of help from their Republican enemies, having dropped the ball on tax reform for two sessions, gave the proposed Palesky tax cap added momentum last spring.

Many Republicans actively welcomed both the Legislative failure and the Palesky initiative as ways to force Governor Baldacci to break his campaign promise of no new broad base taxes. As the 2004 legislative session ended, most state house reporters and many in the political class of both parties were talking about Baldacci's lost leadership and declining political power.

Faced with a gloating MEA and MMA who were poised to garner a windfall of significant proportions, and disillusioned business leaders who had paid for two failed anti-1A campaigns, Governor Baldacci could have thrown up his hands and let matters take their own course.

He did not.

Baldacci was under enormous pressure to have the Tax Cap vote in June when it would have passed easily. He was also under almost desperate demands to come up with a "competing measure" which would simply have ensured the Tax Cap would hang over the NEXT Legislative session. Imagine the lunacy of expecting the Legislature to come with anything of even remote value in a two day summer session!

He did neither.

With the Palesky Tax Cap leading having a 3–1 advantage, John Baldacci stepped up to the challenge and provided much needed strategic guidance, financial backing and tough demands on how to run a winning campaign against the Tax Cap.

He planted his standard on unpopular ground and sought to rally the necessary forces to defeat the ill-advised and draconian Palesky proposal. He said early and often that the Palesky plan was a "meat ax" approach and had to be defeated. Baldacci put his reputation on the line AGAINST a proposition which at the time had a 60% popular appeal simply because he thought it would be bad for Maine.

He showed political courage of the highest order.

In the campaign which followed, many made major contributions:

1. Larry Benoit, Baldacci's former chief of staff, heeded the Governor's plea and came on board to run the day to day campaign. He did a magnificent job. Benoit, along with Kay Rand and Stephanie Clifford, kept the fractious coalition of the MMA, MEA, AFL/CIO and AARP in line and provided a ground game second to none. It was an outstanding performance.

2. Erik Potholm, hired by Benoit over the objections of some partisan Democrats, produced a series of dramatic and powerful 30 second commercials which did not feature a single politician or interest group spokesperson but simply real Maine people whose lives would be negatively affected by the draconian cuts Palesky would have inspired. His first wave of commercials peeled away liberal Democratic votes and many Independents.

3. Martha Freeman, head of the State Planning Office, Jonathan Rubin and Todd Gabe discovered "the kiddie casino" vector of this election cycle, namely the astronomical rises in sales (80%) and income (64%) taxes which would have been required to fill in the gap caused by the cuts in the property taxes. Their contribution proved to be invaluable. Once the second wave of commercials featuring these numbers were shown, conservative urban Franco Democrats and small town Republicans, the two strongest groups favoring Palesky in the summer, turned on the measure with a vengeance. The Yes vote never recovered from these defections.

4. George Smith, perhaps Maine's best known conservative and certainly its most important, broke ranks early with conservative Republicans and wrote a powerful newspaper column indicating why those who wanted tax relief should vote against the tax cap. He made it respectable for conservative Republicans to join the fight against the tax cap. They did so in significant numbers.

5. The Maine State Chamber of Commerce led by Dana Connors, John Oliver and David Brennerman. Faced with strong internal divisions and a business community angry at the lack of legislative action, the Chamber came up with a future spending cap alternative and got behind the Baldacci effort with significant financial and leadership support.

6. Mark Grey, executive director of the MEA, refused to buckle under to NEA and local Maine "wanna-be" kingmaker pressure, and stuck with the local talent that eventually won the referendum for him.

7. Dennis Bailey did his usual superb job of verbally spinning straw into campaign gold and nudged the Maine press corps toward the notion that the Tax Cap was not a guaranteed victory. And his pre-Halloween appearance on television as an aging rock star frightened even the most jaded of Yarmouth yuppies into realizing the end was near.

All of these contributions broke the back of the Yes on One coalition and ensured Governor Baldacci his biggest win yet.

He deserved it.

For the second year in a row Governor John Baldacci led a fight against an initially popular but potentially devastating referendum.

He has proven himself to be a true leader, unafraid to risk defeat for principle, unconcerned about newspaper popularity ratings and unwilling to be deterred by the odds against him.

He is the big winner this November.

THE DYNAMICS OF MAINE'S WELL-BEING

INTRODUCTION

Maine's politics are like its clear, cold January air. Open, honest, bracing. There is no state I know of where the politics are so aboveboard, honest and open to talent. Not everybody ventures out on those crispy, bracing January days with the sky blue beyond belief but those who do, we Mainers stand ready to greet them.

We have much to be thankful for just living in the state of Maine and we can, I believe, take enormous pride in our political culture and be thankful for it. In the section that follows, I have put together some essays which captured for me the essence of Maine.

A WONDERFUL OPPORTUNITY

Only very rarely does an opportunity come along which can revolutionize an entire political system to help it solve fundamental problems. Maine has such a chance right now. Due to changes in the population of its two congressional districts, Maine must redraw the lines of those districts.

The current plan of the Democrats would simply switch some towns such as Waterville from the first District to the second in deference to the two incumbent congressmen. Such a plan would only freeze in place the existing north south split which exists in our state and in fact make the second CD, already the largest district east of the Mississippi, even larger! The Republican plan, however, would create two new districts which would run along a north/south axis instead of its current east/west one.

Thus the state would be divided from north to south with the first CD consisting of such places as York County, all of western Maine and a good bit of northern Maine. It would include Lewiston and Auburn. The second CD would also run north to south and include Portland, Bangor and most of coastal Maine north of York County as well as Aroostook County.

For Lewiston, this new setup would offer substantial advantages: York County and other prosperous locations would have to care about, and do something about, the issues facing northern Maine. Moreover, Lewiston would be in the same district as Biddeford and Saco, thus giving Franco Americans a more powerful voice in its politics. For the citizens of Lewiston and Auburn, this would be a strong step forward and would further enhance the power of Congressman Mike Michaud. He already represents the "tough" part of the state so he would have little problem holding on to his seat.

This new alignment would force policy makers in Washington and Augusta to have to always take into account the essence of one Maine, since both congresspeople would have northern as well as southern Maine in their districts. I believe this would be a huge boon for the northern part of the state and would go a long way to resetting the cognitive map of all of Maine in a positive, constructive, even healthy, way.

Now some Democratic Party stalwarts and their columnist allies have already rejected this plan simply because it is "Republican" and because it would put both sitting Democratic congressmen in the same district. One can only hope that those who truly care about the entire state will override such a shortsighted, partisan approach to our state's problems. Under the new system, no longer could political operatives divide the state into north and south and play off the fears of one against the other. The mistaken notion that Ft. Kent and Saco have nothing in common is precisely what the problem is today and what needs to be rectified.

Other objections seem very weak as well. The U.S. Constitution is quite clear: members of Congress do not have to live in their district, so Congressman Allen and Michaud would not have to move if they wished to continue to represent their current districts. Moreover, the fact that the highly partisan Democratic members of the committee will never agree to it becomes of no consequence since a deadlock will put the competing plans in the courts.

And the courts have ruled the proximity of population totals is the key to a balanced redistricting plan. The Republican plan would put 637,462 people in the first CD and 637,461 in the second. This deviation of 1 person will look extremely good—even unbeatable—to the court. Since 1960, several Supreme Court decisions have ruled that congressional districts within states must be as equal as possible.

For all those concerned about the economic and political splits between northern Maine and the more prosperous south, this is a very rare opportunity to turn around the political culture and the psychographics of the state in one fell swoop.

It is revolution long overdue.

This change will also have one amusing side benefit as well. Should Congressman Allen choose to run in the new second district, he will be forced to pay more attention to the areas outside Portland. Against 30 years of tradition, he previously closed all of his district offices except the one in Portland. In the future, he could not continue to act as if he were still simply mayor of Portland. Just watching him campaign in Calais and Danforth and Madawaska would be worth the price of admission.

NORTH TO "ALASKA"

When I was growing up, my favorite radio show was "Sargent Preston of the Yukon." After 40 years of living happily with my wife, I finally discovered it was one of her favorites as well—although being younger than I, she remembered it as a TV show! Moreover, my wife had always wanted to go on a dog sled ride so for her recent birthday, I took her to Greenville to enjoy Maine's Yukon.

It was a very memorable trip. The dog sled ride was fabulous and for almost two hours, we raced through the woods and along Moosehead Lake, pretending we were in Alaska, going from Dawson to Skagway. The dogs were great and the guide was one of those rural Mainers who inspire both confidence and awe at the way they have put together their lives.

Equally good, we were staying at "The Lodge at Moosehead" where the proprietor, Bruce, upon hearing my sad tale of the freezing bed and breakfast places announced, "You will be sweltering, I guarantee it." He was right. The suite had not one but two fireplaces, including one in the bathroom, and although the outside temperature was −5 degrees, inside it was 90 degrees all night long.

What a treat to have to go out and lie in the snow to cool down.

So it was a wonderful time from beginning to end and well worth waiting for these fifty odd years. But the dogsled guy, Ed Mathieu of Moose Country Safaris, said something very poignant and relevant. We got talking politics and as a man of Franco and Irish descent—and a Republican to boot—he pulled no punches. He had to work four jobs to make ends meet and he was very concerned that his teenage children would have to move away from the state because of the lack of job opportunities. Great Northern Paper had just gone bankrupt that week, and he saw it as only the latest in a long line of downward spiraling economic developments in the region.

"I hope Baldacci doesn't forget about us in the north," he said, "King did, at least the last four years." Now, to be very truthful, I'm not sure what any governor can do by him or herself to change the economic climate.

Because taking a long, winding trip—a big circle to and from Greenville—is a sobering experience in 2003. I hadn't been in that part of the world since the days of Billy Cohen and the U.S. Senate race of 1978, and things seem much, much worse economically. There have been so many plant closings and lost jobs and outmigration of young people, a spiraling down of opportunity that I was truly depressed.

There is something about rural poverty, with all the signs and symbols of broken dreams lying in the dooryard—the rusted machinery, the sagging roofs, bordered up and collapsing buildings—that tears at your heart. The last twenty years has seen the decline of the textile industry, the shoe industry and now the paper and wood industries; so much so that the per capita income for northern and eastern Maine is now $12,000 a year lower than that for southern Maine. That is a terrible gap.

What we need for northern, central and eastern Maine is a Vision Czar, someone who can see the whole picture and put all the pieces together. Tim Woodcock, Bangor's progressive former mayor, would make the ideal Vision Czar. I was very impressed listening to his prescription for the region when I asked him to put my observations in perspective.

He believes we need to look at the region in conjunction with other similar portions New York, New Hampshire, Vermont and Atlantic Canada. This regional approach would enable us to see the role Maine could play in getting goods from Halifax (one of the best ports in North America) and Eastport (a great port but one not connected to first class rail or road nets), to the heartland of the United States.

Moreover, his analysis of the new "pull economy," in which retailers do not ask for products until they have customers for them, requires more and better surface transportation, not less. This suggests that the northern and eastern two-thirds of Maine has an even bleaker future than a past unless it is much better tied into the new American economy.

Part of his solution is the East-West highway which would link Atlantic Canada through northern New England and New York to the expanding markets elsewhere in the United States.

The potential for the Lewiston-Auburn region in this development would be tremendous. The region would be central to the north-south axis of I-95 as well as the east-west axis of the new highway. Instead of paying millions in Tiffs, the region would be highly sought after for its crucial position.

A single column cannot do justice to the scope and depth of his vision, but anyone interested in the future of the region would do well to enlist him in the endeavor to reverse the decline. I've never met anyone with a better grasp of what the future of the region demands.

One final thought about our state's profound problem: no matter how bad the situation has become, the spirit of the people in the region remains unbroken.

Let us hope they get some opportunities to match that spirit.

There may be two Maines in terms of economic development today, but there is only one Maine in our hearts and we owe it to all our citizens to spread out the opportunities and make their futures secure.

"GUNNER" HORNBECK

He's off!

While the rest of us are getting ready for the post Labor Day political campaigns in Maine, the ones dealing with the weighty issues of the proposed gambling casinos as well as tax relief and reform, Richard "Gunner" Hornbeck is flying high above the political storms. Hornbeck, a Richmond resident and Brunswick attorney, is participating in the very prestigious National Air Tour during September 2003. Readers interested in following the actual tour and Hornbeck's role in it can do so on its web site at www.nationalairtour.com.

The National Air Tour of 2003 is a recreation of the last national air tour, scheduled for 1932 but cancelled because of the Depression. It commemorates the 100th anniversary of flight and celebrates an exciting period of aviation. In the 1920's era of "barnstorming," intrepid pilots brought their open cockpit bi-planes and monoplanes to tiny airstrips all across the country, providing thrills and danger for one and all. The earlier National Air Tours were an effort to showcase the best and newest aircraft of the day and introduce them to the American public, to "take aviation to the people" and to promote the building of airports and re-fueling facilities.

I grew up with exciting tales of this era. My father, Harold Potholm, had a bi-plane during this period and thrilled us as children with accounts of open-air cockpit flying—he courted my mother by flying over her house repeatedly. When my father was in his 80's, Dave Smith of Maine Instrument Flight took him over Bar Harbor and let him pilot the plane briefly on the return flight over the sea. It was one of the happiest moments in my dad's later life, but he was always radiant whenever he described the thrill of flying.

That early flying was not all positive and pleasant memories, however, for it could be very dangerous. As a child, it was very sobering, even traumatic, to learn that my uncle Charlie, himself a barnstormer, had died when the wings of his plane fell off as he was putting it into a steep dive in an effort to restore the hearing of a young boy. And my grandfather, so excited after being taken by my father for his first plane ride, jumped out of his seat and ran into the still turning propeller. He died several days later.

The original National Air Tours were sponsored by Ford Motor Company, one of the supporters of this year's recreated tour, and ran from 1925 until 1931. The 2003 version began in Dearborn, Michigan on September 8 and will cover more than 4000 miles and 21 states with scheduled stops in 26 cities. Some of the stops include Minneapolis, Wichita, Tulsa, Ft. Worth, Memphis, Atlanta, Winston-Salem, Pittsburgh, South Bend, Chicago and Milwaukee.

Unscheduled stops will also take place as required for many of the 27 vintage aircraft will need to stop for fuel, mechanical difficulties and the occasional pit stop in between the planned destinations. The flight is planned so that the fastest aircraft leave a location first and the slowest last so that there is no congestion at the arrival point.

These vintage aircraft will include monoplanes, bi-planes and flying boats and their very names are loaded with nostalgia for aircraft buffs: Fairchild (the plane my father learned on), New Standard, Travel Air, Eaglerock, Paramount and WACO.

What makes Hornbeck's participation so special is the fact that he and his co-pilot and navigator Roger Poor, will be flying a 1929 WACO ASO, which Hornbeck has completely restored, literally taking the original aircraft apart piece by piece and putting it back together with loving care and great expense over a 13 year period. I can't imagine flying an open cockpit plane 4000 miles in the first place, let alone trusting yourself to an aircraft you have put back together piece by piece!

Of course, I can barely program my VCR; but still, it seems a magnificent feat when you put the rebuilding and the flying together. I am very impressed with Gunner Hornbeck's accomplishments! They are yet another example of that Maine "can do" spirit with which we can all identify.

"It's both an honor and a challenge," Hornbeck told me in a recent interview. "It's a wonderful chance to be flying with some of the great pilots and great vintage aircraft in America and just to be in that group is a thrill." You could hear the commitment and quiet confidence in his voice and know that 13 years of restoration has given him faith in himself and his aircraft. "I know it will be the experience of a lifetime."

In fact, last year, in order to make sure his aircraft was fit, Hornbeck flew his WACO across the country from Maine to California, and after a quick dip in the Pacific, got back into the plane and flew it back.

How's that for a vision quest?

It makes our daily lives seem pretty ordinary.

We wish all the pilots a great trip and a safe return. And we hope they are mobbed by enthusiastic fans at all their stops.

AN UNEXPECTED JOY

One of the great delights of democracy and its concomitant, bedrock faith in the future is the assumption that your children will, through hard work and application, rise above your station in life. Barry Hobbins' recent column on his son and Little League provoked both nostalgia and gratitude.

Most parents make the assumption that their children can do better in sports or school or socially and advance beyond what they have achieved in life. This is often a bittersweet assumption as time goes on. There is the wonder and joy of their aspirations and the thrill of watching them progress, but also the realization that there are realistic limits as to how far they will progress in sports. No matter how many children want to make it to the Major Leagues or play World Cup soccer, eventually that dream must fade as reality—and other interests—intrude. And few children actually grow up to become president or even senator. This is all part of growing up, of course, but poignant too, for the irony of fate also can play a part.

I was most fortunate when my children were young to have been able to coach them in both baseball and soccer and to watch them far exceed my humble accomplishments on diamond or field. Of course, they had their mother's athletic ability to build on so that was a major plus. I also consider myself fortunate that I was able to transition from coaching my children to climbing up into the stands and letting others coach them as well. There was more than enough reflected glory as Erik made All-State as a goalie and Heather played on Mt. Ararat's state championship team.

But one dream of mine was never fulfilled on the playing fields of Maine. I remember Gordie Howe of National Hockey League fame who stayed around long enough to actually play with his son in the NHL. One summer, I thought I had a chance to play with Erik when he was on a league soccer team, one which occasionally needed additional players when the regulars went on vacation. But when I delicately broached the subject, he realistically replied, "Well, it would be fun but Dad, these guys are big and fast and you really might get hurt."

Now, since I still imagined myself if not 18, then 28, instead of the 48 I really was, it took some time to let reality sink in. He was right, of course, but every once in a while, I had a twinge of regret: it would have been fun to be out on the playing field with your child, even for a short time, in a game that mattered to both of you.

But years later, my dream was realized, although in a somewhat different way and venue. Erik graduated from Colby and went on to graduate school at George Washington and got a master's degree in political management. He specialized in political commercials and was eventually hired by Greg Stevens, one of the premier Republican media gurus in the country. For those of you old enough to remember, he did the ad with Dukakis in the tank with that "What me worry?" look on his face.

Finally, in 1996, when the campaign to widen the Maine Turnpike arrived, and I was in a position to hire the media firm I wanted and designate the account executive, I got to run out onto that field with my son. Despite the inevitable cries of "nepotism," I wanted him on my team because I had seen the commercials he had done and I knew he would be a big asset to our team.

My faith was amply rewarded, for Erik's commercials in the turnpike widening campaign were stunning. They captured the frustrated EMTs and firemen caught in traffic jams on the turnpike and made voters all over the state look on the widening as their need. I remember one 80-year-old man from Bar Harbor saying, "I've got a bad ticker and if I have to go to the hospital, I don't want to get caught in that traffic." These commercials turned the polling numbers around with power and majesty and we won going away.

Even more amazing to me—his old coach—those award-winning commercials had been developed with no input from me. They were his creation and his alone, and they helped me to score a goal on the playing fields of Maine politics. It was then that I realized that Erik was a true and equal partner in the political enterprise game.

Again in 2000, Erik did the commercials for both the forestry referendum and the assisted suicide ballot measure here in Maine. His sets of commercials totally reversed the way people would have voted if they hadn't seen his work. His small woodlot owners unloaded "sprawl" on Jonathan Carter and the NRCM, while his image of the little girl getting suicide pills out of the mailbox sent the National Death Lobby down to defeat.

I now learn more from Erik rather than the other way around. It's a wonderful feeling. For me, to share the joys of political combat turned out to be better than to share the joys of sports combat.

THE DOORYARDS OF BROKEN DREAMS

It is approaching high summer now all across Maine, a welcome respite to the trials of living in the north country for the rest of the year. The wonderful profusion of plants now crowds out, as only Nature can, some of the detritus and debris of our daily lives so visible in other seasons. It no doubt offers for some, the possibility of a future harvest for crops, but in other cases, it simply hides the signs of our failures and diminished dreams as it helps to screen our dooryards of broken dreams.

While urban poverty tends to be concentrated and localized and thus always visible in certain places, rural poverty is widespread and nearly ubiquitous in so many corners of Maine. Somehow, there is also something extra-poignant about seeing it one family, one yard at a time.

Of course, the rural landscape of Maine shows industry and hard work and an independent spirit as well. The earliest settlers, be they Native Americans, or Europeans or later, native born Americans, hacked out livelihoods out of the great wilderness. There are still signs of that struggle and the dreams which succeeded in the hustle and bustle of the small towns and in the easy regularity of the prosperous farming communities.

But rural Maine also contains many—too many—dooryards of broken dreams. As one drives around the state, one sees the signs not just of poverty and hard scrabble living but the decayed and rusted hopes of the past.

They often represent now unrealized and depressing symbols in their "could of, would of, should of" essence.

There are broken snowmobiles and large satellite dishes no longer in use. Assorted farm implements lie rusted and unused here and there. There is a persistent pattern of worn out or discarded machinery as well as junk cars and trucks. There are boats and canoes with holes and boats with no bottoms as well as boats and canoes with weeds growing in them. Power lawn mowers and hand movers no longer useful or useable appear to be almost ubiquitous.

There are unfinished projects, porches with ripped screens, sagging roofs, broken or sagging gutters and other signs of rural decay. Often there are even piles of rotted fire wood, cut with undoubted enthusiasm long ago, but then forgotten or at least left unused until the fiber became rotted and rotten, no longer usable.

If one drives throughout most of western, northern and eastern Maine today, one sees the signs of economic decline everywhere. Almost every major center—Dexter, Milo, Strong, Dover-Foxcroft, Lincoln, Millinocket to name just a few—which once had a textile or shoe factory, wood processing plant or paper mill has lost that facility during the past 30 years.

With those manufacturing plants have gone the highest paying jobs in the entire area as the best jobs have simply gone away. Thirty years ago, when I traveled the second District for then Congressman Bill Cohen, these were thriving, often bustling shire towns, county seats and centers of economic activity. There were significant economic challenges then, of course, but there was hope, hope that government could, should and would do something to make for a better future.

But the last thirty years have witnessed precious little positive political action of a scope necessary to cope with the closures and the reasons for them. For with these closures there have been a series of tremendously debilitating ripple effects coming out of those once prosperous locations. The major industry is gone and with it, the many satellite facilities and small businesses which fed, supplied and distributed those products. Store fronts are vacant, sidewalks cracked and young people leaving. Signs of decline are everywhere. Economic bases have shriveled and withered. A great deal of the quality of life has slipped away for many.

These scenes are not just from some other "other Maine" of dusty economic reports. They are scenes from all over the state. They are not just the broken dreams of others. There is something in the decay and decline that diminishes us all. We are all Mainers and the decline in rural and peri-urban Maine all across the state that lessens the state and both its present and its future for all of us.

Those of us connected to the political world should never forget those dooryards of broken dreams. The dooryards of broken dreams are part of our political as well as our economic reality. It is not enough to blame the Legislature and political leaders. They, after all, give us what we say we want. Too often, in partisan bickering and clashing ideologies, we miss the possibilities of pragmatic solutions which would better the lives of so many.

We in Maine need to refocus our energies in the coming years as we rededicate ourselves to provide meaningful help and opportunity to the working poor who every day confront, often with great courage and resolve, their dooryards of broken dreams. And, as Maria Fuentes puts it, "We must make sure that all the men and women who seek political office really look at those dooryards and care what happens in them."

MAINE: THE WAY LIFE SHOULD BE

For each of us, there may be a different sense of when in time or space the true essence of Maine appears or reappears. For some, it is the Champaign quality of the winter air on a frigid day in January. For others it is that magical May morning when all the buds have popped and "summer" has arrived. Still others are thrilled by the first touch of autumnal breezes in September with the promise of golden leaves. Or it is the first drizzle of snow in November, portending the dazzling change in the landscape of the state.

But each of us also holds, deep within us, a truly powerful sense of what Maine is all about. What in our mindscape, our personal interior landscape, separates it from all the other places we have been in our lives. Whether we were born here or moved here, or moved away but remembered, the essence of Maine remains something very special.

Not only in the mystic cords of our memories, but with each return to the state—whether it is crossing into the country over the Piscataqua bridge, or coming across at Daaquam station, or entering Calais or Eastport, coming out of the mountains through Gilead or Eustis to say nothing of crossing the St. John at its many interfaces with la Belle Canada—one can always recapture that sense of place, of belonging, of coming home into ones own country. For each of us there is a sense that there is something unique about this place, something that truly says, "Maine: The Way Life Should Be."

At most of the entry points into our state, we are greeted by that slogan, a slogan which captures so much of the Maine mystique. It is, as only certain phrases can be, indelible and enduring.

For that, we have David Swardlick of Swardlick Marketing to thank. In the late 1980's, when Maine's Office of Tourism was seeking new directions in its tourist promotion efforts, the slogan was born. Jock McKernan had just been elected governor in 1986 and the new campaign was to begin in 1987.

Swardlick's creative shop was assigned the task of distilling Maine's essence. To discover the summation of what makes Maine unique, what is the true essence of the "Maine mystique." By attempting to define the intangible attributes which Maine people ascribe to themselves and their sense of place, Swardlick and his team used a variety of research tools, including surveys, polling, focus groups and individual interviews.

Their research kept coming back to the same set of aspects: a unique sense that Maine offered something in its quality of life of an almost metaphysical nature, something which transcended region, ethnicity, sex, age and other demographics. People who lived here had it and recognized it, so too did people who had visited the state. It was, in Swardlick's words, "all that is desirable about the state and that which separates it from other places."

Out of that research and creative process came their slogan, "Maine: The Way Life Should Be." The phrase became the centerpiece, the unifying concept for the tourist outreach efforts for the next five or six years. The phrase was to appear on all kinds of promotional material, from brochures and advertisements, to TV and radio commercials to the welcoming signs at many of the entry points into the state.

"Maine: The Way Life Should Be" was initially a perceived attraction to the state, a way to bring people who had never been here, to come here. But in the process, it became something much more enduring, it became our own symbolic referent not that of others. For in truth, according to Swardlick, many people who had never been to Maine simply could not relate to it.

The slogan might make them curious. It might make them want to visit but it did not tell them what there was about Maine that made it "the way life should be." Indeed, for many, the slogan was a not so subtle put-down of where they were already.

Thus over time, the phrase was phased out of state promotional material. But in the meantime, it became something more than a message to lure people to Maine. The slogan was to live on in Maine, adopted by Maine people as a way of describing those intangibles that made of Maine such an attractive place to live, work and visit whether on vacation or not.

Today you see it in editorials, in letters to the editors, in comments on radio and TV shows, in stories and descriptions, even becoming a symbolic referent for behavior as in "This isn't the way life should be." It is now a symbolic referent for what is right and good and the antithesis of anything petty, rude, demeaning and negative.

It has thus become part of our self-image and our sense of collective self-confidence. Who cares if the people in Montana or Georgia don't understand what it means? We do and that is what counts.

So too it is with our being led by men and women who have given of their lives, their treasure and their sacred honor to try to make Maine a better place.

Thanks Dave Swardlick for helping us to see ourselves as we really are.

Although several chapters in this book suggest ways, particularly economic, how Maine's life could be better, even much better, its politics are above reproach. Maine politics are the way political life should be: fair, open to talent, progressive and honest, its hard to argue with the slogan for Maine's political arena.

I hope no one can read the previous chapters without coming to the same conclusion:

Politically, we in Maine are a people blessed.

MAINE IN COMPARATIVE PERSPECTIVE

INTRODUCTION

Much of the rest of the world does not enjoy such an arena as Maine for determining public policy. Most of the nearly 200 entities around the world offer far less opportunities for their citizens to participate and most systems are not polyarchal, let alone true democracies. We take our heritage for granted.

I feel so blessed that my early political career was set in Africa. I did my Ph.D. work on the political development of Swaziland and showed how traditional leadership could survive the onslaught of modernity, contrary to the assumptions of the 1960's. The King of Swaziland still rules 45 years later.

The 1960's were a time of soaring hopes and unprecedented wonder about the delights and possibilities of freedom. Democracy was on the rise. Colonialism was being ended. People were taking charge of their own destinies. It was an exciting time to be out in Africa watching for political change.

Those hopes now lie dashed. Poor political leadership in many places led to a series of keptocracies where the "state" existed only to be looted of treasure. Political systems, always fragile, collapsed and military coups and concomitant corruption became rampant.

Yes the faith of the people endured. Despite everything, wherever there were fair and free elections, the supposedly unsophisticated voters could choose the good over the bad, the well-meaning over the rascals.

Tyrants, petty or grand, soon realized that no matter how poor or "ignorant" the voters, they could tell fraud from performance and the result was, those in charge decided not to have any more elections.

As Americans, we have no idea how fortunate we were that at the inception of the Republic, greed and personal aggrandizement and hatred of democratic processes were not the norm.

Those early political leaders, beset with many problems and centrifugal forces, seemed to have and maintain a vision of the future of America, a future where the government in power, with or without a party apparatus, was not to stay in power forever but that regime alteration was at the very heart of the political system they were passing on to generations yet unborn.

As the following selection shows, we were very blessed and very fortunate. I hope that the pieces which follow help to put that wonderful legacy in perspective. We are bombarded daily with the "problems" in America but very, very few times are these problems put in global perspective and we seldom see paeans of praise for the political system which has stood the test of over 200 years.

We in Maine may stand at the apex of the political system spectrum, be that in the United States or worldwide. We should celebrate our position in the scheme of things, even while trying to improve the workings of our democratic forms.

DR. BANDA

Back when I was teaching and studying African politics, one of my favorite African dictators was Dr. Kamuza Banda of Malawi. Oh there were other tyrants who were more vicious, or who stole more of the people's money or who had greater visions of grandiose grandeur.

But there were few who could rival Dr. Banda when it came to having a tightly wound political system. Initially, Dr. Banda had been prime minister and then president but real elections got tiresome so he had himself made "president for life." That might be enough for most political leaders but Dr. Banda didn't stop there.

He was not anxious to groom a successor and sent into exile a couple of young ministers and vice presidents who, he thought, were eyeing his position. Finally he got tired of that action so he simply did away with the post of vice president. No more vice president—no more second in command waiting to take over. Banda also liked to run the government so he took over the ministries of defense, internal security, agriculture and foreign affairs. In fact, he ran the entire executive branch with an iron hand, holding half of the portfolios himself.

Dr. Banda also appointed all the judges in the country so he controlled the judiciary as well as the executive branch. That left only the legislature. In many African countries, of course, the legislature isn't particularly independent but in Malawi under the good doctor, control of the legislature became a true art form.

Dr. Banda picked all the people who would run for the legislature, the national parliament. Every single one. There was, of course, only one political party, the Malawi Congress Party, and Dr. Banda was the head of it, as well as its national "nominating" committee. This meant he handpicked every member of the parliament giving him total control over the executive, the judiciary and the legislature. Busy man!

So, you say, he was a dictator and ran the country his way. So what? Lots of places are like that. But what I really liked about Dr. Banda was that he held "elections." Not only did he decide when to hold elections and who could run and then, the only permitted newspaper in the country, the *Malawi Times*, faithfully published the results of those "elections" as if they were real. 99% of the people would "vote" and all (100%) would vote for the slate he had picked. Again you say, so what? Lots of communist and other strange forms of government did and do the same thing.

But Dr. Banda was a bit more imaginative than the others. He had the *Malawi Times* publish the results BEFORE the elections were held. Saved a lot of wear and tear on the political process and avoided any suspense (such as a single voter tearing up his or her ballot and thus "spoiling" that vote).

Now in this country, we sometimes don't pay attention to every political story in every paper. But in Malawi, people paid a lot of attention to the results published in the *Malawi Times* because, as you have probably already guessed, Dr. Banda owned the paper as well.

Pretty neat closed political chain I'd say! Not much excitement in the process I'd say.

In terms of predictions, Dr. Banda has thus set a pretty high standard for the *Sun Journal* and this column. But even though it's three weeks to our primary elections here in Maine, already we can announce a number of the "winners" in our races:

The winner of the Democratic primary for governor is John Baldacci.

The winner of the Democratic primary for first CD congressperson is Tom Allen.

The winner of the Democratic primary for U.S. Senate is Chellie Pingree.

The winner of the Republican primary for U.S. Senate is Susan Collins.

The winner of the Republican primary for first CD congressperson is Steve Joyce.

That much we can report at this moment. Pretty neat! We can tell our readers that five of the eight races in Maine political system have already been decided. Bank on it. No surprises, just like in Malawi.

That leaves only three outcomes to be decided which may explain as political junkies our near mania over who is going to win those three, the Democratic race for the second CD nomination, the Republican race for the second CD nomination and the Republican race for the gubernatorial nomination.

Even as I write this, I'm trying to contact Dr. Banda in that big voting booth in the sky to get a line on how those three are going to turn out. When I do get through to him, I'll pass the news on right here in the *Sun Journal*. Weeks in advance if I can.

I'd like you all to know who was going to win all the races before you go to the polls. That would cut down on all the suspense and let the candidates get a good night's rest before Election Day.

WELCOME SOMALIS

The new Somali immigrants being in the news so much recently brought back fond memories of them as people and their marvelous traditional democratic political system. It is too bad that most Americans—and to many Somalis—only know the Somalia of warlords and fighting, of anarchy and deprivation. When I was teaching African politics, they and their political system were one of my favorites. I highlighted them in *Four African Political Systems* (Prentice Hall) and found the Somali people to be proud, innovative, adaptive, tenacious—and very egalitarian.

What most Americans don't realize is that there was a time when the Somali political system was the envy of Africa, a true polyarchal, multi-party democracy with a host of competing organizations and a markedly egalitarian society. It was a unitary state with a National Assembly of 123 members elected by universal adult suffrage. Somalia had an extensive bill of rights, an independent judiciary and democratic processes which started at the local level and worked all the way up to the national forum.

Theirs was a most lively political system and process. For a country of less than three million people, it had over a hundred political parties vying for power. Elections were wide open and exciting. The most important political party was the Somali Youth League (SYL) which led the country to independence and formed the government from 1960 until 1969.

But there was also vibrant opposition provided by the Somali Democratic Union (SDU), the Misbia Destour Mustaquil Somali (HDMS) and the Somali National Congress (SNC) as well as a myriad of other, smaller parties.

For the ten years Somalia was under civilian control, there was thus a very positive, egalitarian, democratic political system which featured two different presidents and four different prime ministers, providing all important regime alteration, a feature seldom seen in sub Saharan Africa. It was a political system, interestingly enough, where when the president of the republic wished to go to the movies, he stood in line with the other patrons. The Somalis would not have it any other way.

Unfortunately, all of this came to a crashing end when on October 15, 1969, a dissident policeman assassinated President Ali Shermarke and the day after his funeral, the Soviet trained military staged a coup, smashing Somali democracy in its infancy. A series of disastrous foreign wars, murderous repression by General Barre, various attempted and successful counter-coups, great power intervention, political and economic fragmentation, regional secession and finally, violent civil war shattered the Somali political system and brought long term chaos.

The Somalis who are now arriving in the area have had to deal with all of the above. They have had decades of trauma and deprivation. Their misery is difficult to describe because it was so bad and went on for so long.

Now the Somalis want to start a new life. Theirs is the American dream. Like so many other immigrants, they come to America with high hopes and aspirations; they come for safety, security, and an all-important chance at a better life. Like the English and Scots, Irish and Germans, Italians and French, Chinese and Indians, Koreans and Spanish, Mexicans and Vietnamese, Cambodians and Afghanis, they come to America to make something of themselves and add to the rich vibrant steam that is our country's history, our present and, hopefully, our future.

My maternal grandmother, Anna "Nana" Carlson arrived in America in the late nineteenth century from her native Sweden. She told me of her childhood and that, as a teenager, she worked on a big estate as a maid and often had only a single hard-boiled egg to eat for her meals. She had started work when she was only nine years old.

Life was desperately poor and for people of her social and economic status, likely to remain so for the rest their lives. She was born into a trap where there could be no viable dream for her tomorrows. There was no future for her in the country of her birth. So she and her family risked everything and braved the unknown to come to America. Passing the Statue of Liberty, she wept and said: "This is my home now."

Coming to America was, she always believed, a dream come true because in America everybody's dreams *could* come true. America is still a dream come true and we should welcome the Somalis with open arms, remembering that we and our ancestors arrived here in the same situation as they.

In some cases we were welcomed and some we were not. It is better when America is welcoming. We all gain from the process and America is a richer place for the efforts of those who come here and those who welcome them.

Pat Buchanan once said that it was "easier to integrate a person of English extraction than a Zulu" into the American political, economic and social systems. Now in some rudimentary sense, of course, he is correct. It's always easier to integrate people from similar backgrounds and heritages. But what a dull and sterile America it would have been if only the English had come to our shores, and only they had been allowed to be integrated into our political system.

Let us reach out to the Somalis and the future others who will continue to see America the land of promise and the land of plenty and for in doing so, we add to the many, many glorious facets of our total national heritage.

Let us welcome them the way we would have wished our ancestors to be welcomed.

We were all Somalis once.

"41" AND "43"

The recent Bush fundraising event at the Black Point Inn in Scarborough was quite an affair. It was, quite simply, the largest fundraiser in the history of the Republican Party in Maine. For Sandy and me, there was also an overwhelming sense of déjà vu in the hot sunlight with the Republican faithful filling several huge tents on the edge of the Gulf of Maine.

It reminded us of a similar gathering 11 years ago at Walker's Point when President George Bush (now known to Republican faithful as "41") hosted a similar affair. Same type of gorgeous day looking like a Luminist painting, same fired-up Republicans, same quiet sense of "God's in his heaven, all's right with the world."

The protesters there even seemed the same!

Back in 1991, of course, we had commenced Operation Desert Shield (which would six months later become Operation Desert Storm) and there was opposition to our policy toward Iraq. Last weekend there were a dozen or so protestors standing against America's plans to attack and oust Saddam Hussein.

There was also a small Green party contingent for Jonathan Carter. You remember Carter? He was supposed to have an impact on this year's governor's race but he seems to have taken the summer off. At least I don't see him on TV.

What struck me about this year's gathering of over 500 Republicans on that hot August Saturday was their obvious enthusiasm for the statewide ticket. I don't ever remember when so many Republicans were so excited about the total ticket. They cheered Collins and loved her rock-steady position in the polls. They cheered Peter Cianchette as he continues to close in on Baldacci and they thought the two congressional candidates, Kevin Raye and Steve Joyce were the most formidable in years. They especially like the way Joyce is getting under the skin of their old nemesis, Tom Allen.

And, no matter what the state of Maine has—or has not—done electorally for Bush senior and Bush junior, hard core Republicans love them both. "41" was greeted like a rock star when he entered the tent, man and women surging up to him to say hello and to touch him. There had been palpable excitement as the word spread that "41" was driving "43" (sometimes also known as "Quincy" to complete the presidential history references to John Adams and John Quincy Adams, the only other father and son combination in history) to the event in the senior Bush's speedboat, the Fidelity II.

"43" was at the top of his game. Bouncy, combative and charming, he wowed the audience. For those who only see him on TV, sometimes looking as if he's seen the script for the first time, he's very different in person. He looks and acts like a winner. He was very laudatory toward Susan Collins, listing her many contributions to our national political life and praising—somewhat playfully—her independence and feistiness: "I don't do everything she says. She doesn't do everything that I say." Standing between two presidents, the candidate beamed. Independent, feisty and committed, she's the Republican's new Margaret Chase Smith.

Interestingly enough, beyond the great cheers for the various Republican candidates, the audience most appreciated "43's" references to hunting down and bringing to justice the terrorists and his promise to permanently repeal the death tax. I believe an objective observer would say the death tax reference won the ovation contest.

Having been to a lot of Republican fundraising events over the years, it's pretty easy to become jaded and cynical. But this year seems different. The Republicans feel both embattled and righteous. They love the feel and tone and ethics of this administration after the Clinton years and they are very buoyed over the possibility of retaking the Blaine House and holding on to the Congress.

They know it won't be easy.

There was lots of talk about the tons of national Democratic soft money pouring into the state and their reported 30 political operatives going door-to-door in an attempt to revive the flagging candidacy of Chellie Pingree. But there are hosts of young Republicans ready to take up the challenge.

Major players (such as the always impressive Daryn Demeritt) and worker bees abounded and the next generation of Republican "young guns" was very much in evidence and ready for battle. Jason "Jedi in Training" Fortin, Jeff Morris, Jeff Tulley, Billy Thompson, Kati Horsman, Collee Frawley, Pat Woodcock and James Stearns all looked primed. Some Republican insiders are already saying "Jimmy S" Stearns will soon be ready to challenge the legendary Democratic operative, "Jimmy B" Betts.

I was also very impressed with the organization and logistics of the event. Hosting 500 people is never easy and especially with town and state and secret service security, it could have been hellish. Steve Abbott, Randy Bumps, Jan Staples, Ken Burrill and Jeanne Little, among others, did a great job pulling it all together. Felicia Knight did her usual fine spinning and Cynthia Bergman also helped the press to stay focused on the issues that matter. Bergman is becoming a real asset to the Republicans this cycle.

Whether Republican or Democrat, Green or Reform, these type of gatherings for the party faithful never fail to give me hope for the future of our political system. So few people ever bother to get involved with politics enough to show up at affairs like this, it's always stimulating to see the few that do getting ready for the next battle.

We in Maine are very fortunate this election cycle. We have four major contested races and a huge amount of national interest in the Maine outcomes.

Nobody in the state has an excuse to sit on the sidelines this time.

WE WERE SO BLESSED

The attempts at nation-building in Iraq have once again cast into sharp relief the difficulties in getting—and holding—a national consensus among competing ethnic, regional or ideological groups and in establishing a democratic or even quasi-democratic political system.

Since the decolonization spurt which began in 1946 in the Sudan and on the Indian subcontinent in 1947, there have been hundreds of attempts to make democratic polities endure and prevail. The track record of those attempts makes grim and depressing reading. While there have been almost as many explanations as observers, few have focused on what to me is truly the heart of the matter.

Ayi Kwa Armah, author of the profoundly moving and perspicacious novel, "The Beautiful Ones Are Not Yet Born," however is one. Armah, the Ghanian novelist, pinpoints the awful truth that when you look closely at the failures in the developing world, colonialism, heightened ethnicity, religious strife and all the rest—while contributing factors—are not the decisive cause of failure to build a viable political system and nation.

Rather, the chief failure lies in the inability or unwillingness of the political elite to do what is in the nation's best interest, not simply their own or their political base's. It is precisely this failure of leadership that has destroyed functioning democratic systems in some countries and prevented their creation in others.

In our history, we have the monumental failure of political leadership in the 1850's that led to the greatest national trauma in our history, the Civil

War. Many have seen the Civil War as a historical struggle between different ways of life, of military process writ large or by an inevitable clash of the highest moral order. But in fact, it was the failure of the political elites to work within the democratic framework already established to prevent the war and solve the basic question of slavery and stave off political decay.

So we Americans are not without political sin or bad examples. But where we were extraordinarily blessed was in the critical formative years from 1776 to 1783, in the early days of the Republic when basic decisions were made by the political leadership which however diminished by retrofitting contemporary values onto those leaders, saved the American democratic experience from being still born or the victim of infanticide by regional, ideological or personal whim.

George Washington, Thomas Jefferson, James Madison, John Adams, Alexander Hamilton and others, despite their petty differences and jealousies, when it really mattered, put in the background their personal interests and aspects in order to form "a more perfect union." As the father of his country, George Washington could have been elected president again and again, even president "for life" as so many African dictators did. Thomas Jefferson or John Adams or Alexander Hamilton could have made decisions that could have split the early Republic into fragments or narrowed rather than broadened participation in, and commitment to, the idea of being "an American."

We often forget that those formative years between 1776 and 1783 were fraught with danger, there was no guarantee that "America" as we know it, was designed to survey the growing pains of its birth. We pass over, far too lightly, the dangers of Shay's and Whiskey rebellions, separatist tendencies, foreign intrigue and the threat of European war as well as the opportunity for the early presidents to grab more power and wealth at the nation's expense and put centrifual forces against the fragile unity of the nation. The transition between the "no-party" first term of Washington and the emerging dual party system (Federalists versus Republicans, later the Democrat-Republicans) was fraught with danger for the new nation.

As Professor Jean Yarbrough points out, the election of 1800 is a good case in point. With the House of Representatives deadlocked after 35 votes for president, Alexander Hamilton, a Federalist, threw his support behind Thomas Jefferson, a Democrat-Republican, the first peaceful transfer of power from one party to another in our history. This feat has seldom been duplicated in the majority of over 150 countries in the world. A peaceful power transition remains one of the most important benchmarks of functioning democracy.

The "mild solution" of 1800 remains a true rarity.

So much of recent revisionist American history focuses on the shortcomings of our early democracy—slavery, property qualifications and denial of the vote for women—that we often overlook the enormous leap of political faith made during our early Republic and what an enduring beacon of political hope we truly created.

The early leaders of America may have been propertied white males with elitist attitudes, but luckily they were "The Beautiful Ones" when we needed them to be.

For the initial American political system, "The Beautiful Ones" were born and born at the right time.

It is a blessing we often forget but shouldn't.

ONE WORD MORE

GIVING THANKS

As we end 2005, many of us look back on the things we should have done and try to do them before the new year arrives. In my case, I have long wanted to do a column this year about how thankful I am for all the men and women who are in and around Iraq serving in our armed forces, but especially those from Maine.

No matter what one's views on the war itself, or the administration which began it or the difficulties in seeing it through to a positive conclusion, we all should underscore our appreciation for those who are far from home and sacrificing their time, their treasure and even their lives to make our own safer. They deserve our strongest support and most heart-felt appreciation.

This is true for those men and women in the regular army, navy, air force, marines and coast guard as well as those Maine based Army National Guard. In addition to the 133rd Engineer Guard unit recently in the news after the attack in Mosul, there are Maine members from the 304th Regiment, the 619th Transportation Company and the 152nd Field Artillery Battalion as well as crew members from the U.S. Coast Guard Cutter Wrangell and the VP Navy Patrol Squadron and those recently called up for active duty like the 152nd Maintenance Company scheduled to go to Iraq in January. I apologize in advance if I have inadvertently missed any of the Maine units deployed.

It is particularly heart-wrenching to see mothers and fathers, sons and daughters and even grandfathers and grandmothers being uprooted from friends, family and normal life to go abroad to a hostile land in the middle of a vicious insurgency.

Especially around the holidays their departures and tribulations seem particularly poignant. Loved ones know their own sacrifices as they serve and often continue to serve beyond their prescribed tours of duty. Whether through poor planning on the part of our leadership or changed circumstances, the need for their ongoing service continues as we enter 2005.

During the Vietnam War, the National Guard served many important functions and purposes, but its members did not generally serve overseas in combat. One of the major post-war reforms in the military was to fully integrate the National Guard into the regular armed forces and make sure that the Guard could and would be used wherever and whenever needed. The swift and decisive conclusion of the Gulf War of 1991 seemed to indicate just how well that adjustment had worked.

But the major shrinkage of the total American armed forces following the end of the Cold War has meant that the United States military has had to depend more and more on the National Guard for protracted wars or peace keeping efforts. The results have been painful. Lives are disrupted, families separated and the harsh realities of a long-term war casts a long psychological and physical toll. The strains seem almost palpable and is becoming harsher as personnel are deployed over and over and for longer periods.

As the United States pursues the global war on terror and faces an increasing arc of instability from collapsed and failed states which cannot police their own borders nor control their own countries, a major expansion of the regular armed forces (and a much needed rebalancing of the new needs within those regular armed forces) will be required. We have found out, unfortunately, that many of our "allies" in Europe and the UN cynically refuse to help stabilize the situation and want only for us to fail. I think of Kosovo with some bitterness since Europe was unable to stop the fratricide and the UN was paralyzed, leaving us to do the bulk of the work.

Fighting global terrorism will not be an easy or quick task. The campaign rhetoric about a reinstated draft completely misses the point of twenty-first century warfare. The Pentagon does not want a draft. Given the demands of warfare, especially command and control today, a draft simply would not provide the necessary high quality of recruits to master both the technology and the far more vigorous training of small unit cohesion. We need to expand the all-volunteer force as quickly and judiciously as possible but that requires higher benefits and will take a good deal of time to implement.

In the meantime, we should focus our praise, our hopes and our thanks on the men and women from Maine and elsewhere who have disrupted their lives and even paid the ultimate sacrifice to keep us and our way of life secure.

Our debt to them is enormous.

Without them, we would be unprotected and our precious freedoms would melt away.

REFERENCES

Some of these essays, several under different titles and several in a slightly different form, originally appeared in *The Sun Journal*, except where noted below:

"Reality Check," ("Potential Candidates Get Reality Check"), June 10, 2001; "Uzi Suzie," July 1, 2001; "Statesman?," ["Is Bennet a Statesman?,"] (July 22, 2001); "Time Speeded Up by Events," (Aug. 19, 2001); "In Praise of Virgins," ["A Serious Contender Emerges,"] (Sept. 16, 2001); "Here Comes the Judge," (Nov. 4, 2001); "There Goes the Judge," (Nov. 16, 2001); "A Sinking Ship?," ["Is the Ship Sinking?,"] (Jan. 6, 2002);

"A Whole New Ballgame," Feb. 10, 2002; "The Ides of March," (Mar. 3, 2002); "Vox Populi," ["Vox Populi: 'The Voice of the People,"] (Mar.31, 2002); "Campaign in 3D," ["It's a 3-D Race for Governor,"] (Apr. 21, 2002); "Dr.Banda," ["Message from Dr. Banda,"] (May 12, 2002); "Welcome Somalis," ["Somalia Was Once a True Democracy,"] (May 26, 2002); "Vindication," ["A Key Stroke of Genius,"] (July 21, 2002); "'41' and '43'," ["Summer of '41' and '43',"] (Aug. 18, 2002); "The Perfect Storm," ["Pumped-Up Coffers Leading to Blitz of Local Political TV Ads,"] (Sept. 29, 2002); "Elections and the Role of Biography," (October 27, 2002), "I Was Wrong," (Nov. 10, 2002); "A Grand Moment," ["A Historic Moment for the State of Maine,"] (Dec. 8, 2002); "Bed and Political Breakfast," (Jan. 5, 2003); "A Wonderful Opportunity," (Mar. 30, 2003); "Behold the Psychographics," ["Psychographics:

It's All in the Mind,"] (Oct. 12, 2003); "Some Who Mattered," (Nov. 9, 2003); "Ode to John," *The Times Record* (Jan. 17, 2003); "North to 'Alaska,'"(February 2, 2003); "Gunner Hornbeck" ("Biplane Adventurer Sparks Fond Memories," (September 14, 2003); "An Unexpected Joy," (August 17, 2003); "A Cascade of Ironies, (April 25, 2004); "Everybody Won?," (December 7, 2003); "Maine: The Way Life Should Be, (July 18, 2004).

ABOUT THE AUTHOR

Chris Potholm is the author of 14 books, including *This Splendid Game*, *The Delights of Democracy* and *An Insider's Guide to Maine Politics*. He is De Alva Stanwood Alexander Professor of Government at Bowdoin College and has been active in politics as a pollster and strategist for over 30 years.